CLASSIC
SCANDINAVIAN
COOKING

CLASSIC
SCANDINAVIAN
COOKING

NIKA HAZELTON

Galahad Books
New York

Published in 1994 by

Galahad Books
A division of Budget Book Service, Inc.
386 Park Avenue South
New York, NY 10016

Galahad Books is a registered trademark of Budget Book Service, Inc.

Published by arrangement with Macmillan Publishing Company, Inc.

Library of Congress Catalog Card Number: 86-14621

ISBN: 0-88365-856-9

Printed in the United States of America.

FOR MÅLFRID STENERSON

CONTENTS

CLASSIC
SCANDINAVIAN
COOKING

INTRODUCTION

The purpose of this book is to acquaint home cooks with one of the world's most pleasant and satisfying cuisines, as well as to give recipes that are traditional and authentic yet feasible in our kitchens. Classic Scandinavian food is excellent, real, honest food, easily adaptable to any occasion. It is liked not only by grownups, but also by fussy children. What more can one ask of a foreign cuisine?

Scandinavia, the most northern part of Europe, consists of five countries, namely Denmark, Norway, Sweden, Finland, and the northern island in the Atlantic, Iceland. Like a family, Scandinavia is worth getting to know as a unit and then again for its individual members. Each of the Scandinavian countries is worth visiting for its own charms, be they nature, art, food, or people. Since this is a cookbook, I shall talk about the food of Scandinavian countries, which has a lot in common from country to country, with some differences due to varied natural resources and historical background. I am talking of the classic, traditional food, but let us not forget the egalitarianism of modern living found in almost every part of the world. Gastronomically speaking, Denmark and Sweden have the finest and most varied and appealing food. Both countries have a past of rich and splendid courts, whose tastes filtered down into the population; they also had the natural resources, such as meats and dairy products, for fine dishes. Finland, an independent country only since 1917, shares both a Swedish and Russian upper-class food tradition with the rustic native fare; Finland was ruled at different times by Sweden and Russia. The traditional foods of Norway are those of a poor, rustic country, though this does not make them less tasty. The food of Iceland is basically in the Norwegian tradition; Iceland, like all of Scandinavia, is by no means poor, but it is still a small island and not so abundantly endowed as some of the other Scandinavian countries.

Whatever the differences, you'll always eat well in Scandinavia. The food is nicely prepared and served, even in places where groups of tourists are accommodated. This is not true, alas, of quite a few countries that I could name, as the saying goes.

Wherever you are in Scandinavia, you're never far from the sea or lake or stream, meaning that fish was—and still is— found in all Scandinavian cooking, and Scandinavia is justly famous for its extremely fresh and wonderfully tasting fish and its fish cookery. Fish was cheap and nourishing, and fishing a major mainstay of the economics of Norway and Iceland. But commercial fishing is hard work and nearby waters do not yield as much as they once did. The high standard of living, the welfare state, and changing tastes promoted by travel—in short, modern life—has lessened the importance of fish in the Scandinavian home diet, and has seen an increase in the consumption of meat. But here again, not all of Scandinavia is alike; in Denmark, a well-to-do agricultural country, fish was never nearly as much a staple of the diet as in Norway. In any case, all, or almost all Scandinavian fish recipes are very good, and the fish you eat there is much fresher than any available in this country, barring the fish you are lucky enough to catch and cook the same day.

Since the original edition of this book appeared, the world, including Scandinavia, has changed its ways of living. We are entering a new age of technology. Women working outside the home, less housekeeping, new appliances such as microwave

ovens, widespread travel, fast foods, low-paid immigrant labor-
ers and their ethnic ways, electronics, politics have produced
changes all over the world—nowhere more than in the United
States. Scandinavia is affected by all of these changes. Generally
speaking, World War II changed a great deal of Scandinavia,
removing it from the forefront of social progress and beautiful
design. The welfare state is no longer typically Scandinavian,
and Scandinavian design, so long admired as the greatest and
most advanced, fell behind because of changing times, imitations,
and the like; stainless steel is in use instead of Danish silver flat-
ware, and Asian designs are found more frequently than Finland's bold Marimekko patterns. Art Deco is preferred to chaste
teak furniture, and frozen food is more popular than canned.
Above all, before World War II, for historical and cultural
reasons, Scandinavia had felt kinship with Germany, and German was the foreign language one learned. Now, however,
English is the second language and Scandinavia is looking, like
almost all of the world, to America.

Food and eating habits are a part of this change, though it
is not nearly as far-reaching, faddish, or rapid as in the United
States.

In all of the Scandinavian countries, people are more nu-
trition conscious than they were. They diet, they eat more vegetables and fruits and fewer dairy products, they go to exotic
foreign restaurants—in short, they are in a transition period
where their food and food habits are concerned. Yet, in spite of
the wealth produced by the tourist trade, for which all the Scandinavian countries angle like mad, there is still a respect for
tradition in food and ways of living. There is little of the casual
dropping in of friends which Americans take for granted, taking
potluck or bringing food. Except for family and some extremely
close friends, one entertains mainly by invitation though ethnic
foreigners and the admirers of American informality are far

more open to having outsiders in their homes. Since entertaining means more and more elaborate food than daily family fare, now that so many women work outside the home and there is less time for cooking, a great deal of hospitality has been transferred to the ever-proliferating restaurants.

One of the great differences of Scandinavian life was—and still is—meal times. In order to make the most of the precious free times, especially the long and bright summer evenings, Scandinavians ate their main meal of the day as soon as they came home from work. To start the day, breakfast was quite substantial, including cheese, cold meats, pickled herring, maybe boiled eggs—whatever your taste and your standard of living considered a substantial meal. Lunch consisted of a cup of coffee and a simple sandwich eaten at work. Then, in the afternoon, generally between four and seven o'clock, you ate your *middag*, your main meal. After your afternoon pursuits, in the evening, you had a snack. The advantage of this mealtime schedule is that it lets you have a good deal of free time in one piece, especially for the summer months, but modern life has been eroding the sensible way of living. I imagine that eventually it will disappear like the siesta, the sensible habit in hot climates, when you take a rest during the hottest hours of the day. However, traditional Scandinavia shows pity for hungry people. Even before the event of fast foods and supermarkets, you could find *konditoris* combining coffee shops and pastry shops (the pastries are generally very rich, creamy, and utterly delicious) and stands where hot dogs, smaller and tastier than ours, are sold. And if you see the words *is* or *glass* on a stand, you will find ice cream there; even Scandinavian Viking types, below and above the Arctic Circle, cannot resist ice cream.

One of the joys of a cuisine still unfamiliar to us is the desserts. This, I can say with a heartfelt emphasis, is very, very true of Scandinavian cooking. Scandinavian desserts are infinitely more appealing than our desserts. Soufflés, tortes, fruits combined with pure, superlatively fresh whipped or poured thick cream are totally irresistible even to those of us who usually, for our own reasons, do not eat desserts. They are rich, though maybe a shade less so than in the old days, as is all modern food, but they are worth every bite.

And, in season, do not neglect the berries, served, as they should be, with cream. Berries do well in cool climates—I never ate better strawberries than in northern Norway, above the Arctic Circle, grown there in their short summer season. Among the most delicious and unique-tasting aromatic berries are the cloudberries that grow in northern Norway, Sweden, and Finland. They look like an oversized unripe raspberry, pale golden in color, and are called *multer* in Norway, *hjortron* in Sweden, and *lakka* in Finland. The Finns make a delightful liqueur out of their juice. If you cannot eat fresh cloudberries, I strongly recommend buying them canned or frozen in any food shop that carries Scandinavian imports.

As for nonalcoholic drinks, Scandinavians are coffee drinkers, rather than tea drinkers. Good strong coffee, big cups of it, hot and made exclusively with coffee beans, is the beverage of Scandinavia, though necessity at times has forced substitutes, especially in Denmark and Norway, where coffee has been very expensive at times.

Scandinavians, people of the north, like to drink strong waters. Their typical drink is akvavit (which translates as "water of life"), commonly known as *snaps*. Traditionally, a shot glass of icy akvavit is taken at the beginning of the main meal of the day, followed by a beer chaser—Scandinavian beer is excellent and it is drunk by people of all ages. The reason for this, I gather, is that combination of the warming quality of the *snaps* and its affinity for the tidbits of smorgasbord and open sandwiches. Besides, grapes do not grow in cold Scandinavia, but the potatoes and grains used to make akvavit do—ergo, akvavit is the national firewater. Akvavit, to put it mildly, is an extremely powerful drink, and tossing it down, as we know the Russians toss down their vodka, will reduce the unsuspecting foreigner to pulp. Akvavit has never gained a foothold outside Scandinavia and the Baltic and North Sea coasts. However, Sweden and Finland have gone into the international markets with their vodkas. Scandinavia traditionally also produces some pleasant fruit wines and liqueurs made largely from berries.

Drunkenness has always been a problem in Scandinavia, in spite of stringent liquor laws, temperance movements, state monopolies on imported wines and spirits, and the high cost of liquor.

There is no native cocktail hour in the lands of the north, unless the natives are living like Americans. At best you may get a pre-dinner glass of sherry or an apéritif before settling down at the table to serious eating and drinking. Here the drinking ritual begins, and it is a lot of fun, especially for the female visitor, who likes to gaze long and deeply into handsome, reciprocating Nordic eyes.

This ritual has some slight variations, but here is the basic procedure, which will see you through. Never lift your glass to your lips or, worse, drink first. Listen closely to the word *skål* or *skol*, which comes after your host has spoken his *velkommen til bords*, which means "welcome to the table." When you hear the magic word, grasp your glass and bring it up slightly north of the region of the heart. But do not let your lips touch it yet. As a guest, you will be looked at, by your host, with a purposeful, magnetic stare, glass raised (in Sweden they used to say at the level of the third button of the uniform). Then you drink simultaneously, and regardless of whether you are very experienced or very inexperienced, you toss it down with a gulp. Then you return your glass south of your chin, from where it came, glance again into your skoaler's eyes, nod your head around the table in a rather stately manner, deposit your glass and reach for your beer to quench the fires of the akvavit. The same procedure applies to wine, but not to beer.

When the urge for another drink seizes you, take the initiative in a bold manner—don't forget the word *skål* as you repeat the ritual. You yourself can *skål* anybody as often as you want or as long as the going is good, and earn the gratitude of your fellow diners. But you can't *skål* your hostess as often as you want, presumably because somebody has to keep her wits about her, though she can *skål* you to her heart's content.

Now this ritual, described in print, sounds complicated, just as the process of breathing sounds complicated if you try to describe it in detail. In reality, Scandinavian drinking is as easy as breathing, and takes practically no practice at all. A couple of drinks and you're there, skoaling as naturally as you put food in your mouth. It's a very pleasant practice, in more ways than one, as many a lad or lass gazing his way through Scandinavia will tell you.

In spite of the advantages and disadvantages of modern day life in Scandinavia, its countries are full of wonders of every kind. Above all, the food is excellent, especially the traditional dishes. And you will find in Scandinavia an honest and sympathetic approach, a courtesy and helpfulness not easily found anywhere else in the world.

HOW TO FREEZE
A BOTTLE OF AKVAVIT IN ICE

Akvavit must be served ice cold, but no ice must ever touch the actual drink. The simplest way of chilling a bottle of akvavit is to stand it in the refrigerator for a day or two, or until it is thoroughly chilled. In restaurants the akvavit bottle is often encased in a block of ice, which seems a complicated magic trick and impossible to achieve at home. Not so at all; all that is needed is a freezer and a large tin can about 8 inches tall and 3 inches larger in diameter than the akvavit bottle. You may also use an emptied, ½-gallon milk carton.

First, freeze about ½ to 1 inch of water in the bottom of the can or carton. Then place the akvavit bottle on the ice, in the center of the container. Add cold water almost to the top. Place container in the freezer and make sure that the bottle remains dead center.

When the water surrounding the akvavit bottle is thoroughly frozen, dip the can quickly into hot water; the bottle in its coating of ice is then easily removed. If using a carton, simply tear away the container. Serve by holding the bottle with a napkin and pouring the akvavit into thimble-sized glasses.

ABOUT THE RECIPES

Scandinavian food is wonderful, and best of all it appeals to the basic American taste for flavor and substance. Since it would have been impossible to include every excellent dish, I have chosen those I consider both representative of traditional Scandinavian cooking and of interest to the American home cook.

Unquestionably, traditional Scandinavian food is, generally speaking, richer than other cuisines. Where possible, the recipes have been tailored to reduce fat, sugar, etc., without sacrificing taste. I would suggest adapting these recipes to the tastes, food habits, and needs of those being served. I imagine you will want more substantial food in the cold of a northern midwestern winter than if you live in the South. The recipes take into consideration that even traditional cookery has been modernized. But when it comes to baked goods and other desserts, I suggest that the cook use the recipes as they appear in this book. Scandinavian baking may be rich, but it is very festive. Try a cookie or cake recipe as it is shown when you first make it, and do your adapting after.

Quantities. This depends on the use to be made of the dishes. Obviously, for example, if you plan to use a salad to make a Danish open-faced sandwich, you will need to make less of it than if it is to be part of a smorgasbord or used as a main course. Quantities also depend on the number of people to be fed and on their appetite. To be on the safe side, the recipes generally follow the customary 4 to 6 servings.

Recipe Names. Since Scandinavian recipes frequently resemble each other, I have used their specific names in the language of the country where I was told by Scandinavian cooks they originated.

SMORGASBORD
AND
SMØRREBRØD

Smorgasbord, literally a table covered with buttered bread, is the Scandinavian tradition Americans are most familiar with. Alas, the table groaning under dozens of little dishes—containing bits of almost everything edible in nature, home grown, raised, fished, or imported—does exist today only in the fanciest restaurants, mainly in Sweden, that cater largely to affluent foreign tourists. But more frugal souls can find simplified versions. Smorgasbord is really nothing but an assortment of as-many-as-you-like appetizers, like its kissing kin, the Russian *zakuski*, which are tossed down with vodka. If you are planning to make a meal of smorgasbord, usually followed by dessert, eat as much of it as you want to. But if you want a main dish in your meal, go easy on the smorgasbord.

Smørrebrød (the word *smørre* means "butter" and *brød* means "bread") is the Danish version of the smorgasbord of Sweden. Smorgasbord is known as *Koldt bord* in Denmark. The difference between the two is that smørrebrød consists of open-faced sandwiches piled high with assorted tidbits, while in the smorgasbord similar foods are served in dishes or on platters. Smørrebrød is a way of life in Denmark, but Americans, used to the covered sandwich, think of it as a foreign delicacy. Smørrebrød is, like smorgasbord, a convenient way to make tidbits go a long way, besides being very decorative if you are neat and have an eye for attractive foods, as do the Danish people.

Both smorgasbord and smørrebrød, fancy or simplified, lend themselves very well to our American way of life. Either one can be as abundant or restricted as the occasion and the hosts' circumstances demand. And last but not least, a nice smorgasbord or smørrebrød will convince everyone that you think and care about food.

HOW TO SET UP A SMORGASBORD FOR A BUFFET PARTY

A smorgasbord is an exellent way of entertaining a group of people, since it is easily planned and prepared in advance.

The first thing a hostess preparing a smorgasbord should do is to take a trip to a good Scandinavian or food specialty store. Specialty food stores can be found in department stores, and many supermarkets have gourmet corners with foods suited to a smorgasbord. At the store, you should pick up several varieties of canned herring and other imported canned fish. These are an integral part of the smorgasbord, and besides, this is what the Scandinavian cook would do. Nobody expects a home cook to produce the almost endless variety of canned fish found on a smorgasbord.

Then, since the sky is the limit at a smorgasbord, you should choose a grand assortment of other foods. If the aim is to have an authentic feast, you might choose the goodies imported from Scandinavia. The idea of a smorgasbord is to have variety, as well as foods that are not usually eaten at home, and the more of these the merrier.

The next step is to give some careful thought to the arrangement. This is extremely important, because a good smorgasbord is also to be looked at. Apart from the decorative aspects, the foods must be arranged in a neat, orderly manner, so they can be eaten in their proper order, that is, in courses, beginning with fish. The best way to arrange a smorgasbord is on a long table, where the different kinds of dishes can be laid out in rows and in a related order.

The table, to look authentic, should be laid with a white cloth. Color is provided by flowers and accessories, such as candles, set at either side of the table toward the back, and the figurines so often found on Swedish tables. At one end of the table the plates, silverware, and napkins are placed. There must be enough plates so that each guest can have a clean one for each course—the fish course, the meat and salad course, and the warm course. The plates need not be as large as dinner plates, but if you do not have enough of them to last through the smorgasbord, they will have to be washed in between. It is absolutely essential to have clean plates for each course. The same goes for the silver, and if paper napkins are being used, there should also be several changes of these.

At the opposite end of the table, on hot trays and over candle warmers, are the hot dishes, such as meatballs, egg-and-anchovy dishes, creamed potatoes, etc.

The foods can be arranged either in rows or in related groups. If the smorgasbord is to be an American one—that is, a complete meal—it should include coffee, cake, and cookies. These are best arranged on a separate table, such as a card table laid with a white cloth.

Every smorgasbord must include several kinds of bread, such as white, light and dark rye, and pumpernickel (all these should be firm), Swedish rye crisp, and Norwegian flat bread. There should be plenty of butter, shaped into rolls or curls, and each little butter dish should be garnished with a sprig of fresh parsley. And don't forget several kinds of cheese, served in large chunks.

Making the food look attractive is as important as making it taste good. The canned fish need not be removed from the containers, but the cans should be opened and the lids rolled back neatly to show the contents. Each can should be set on its own little plate, and the plate garnished either with a lettuce leaf, a few dill sprigs, radish rosettes, or lemon slices—anything that will make a can look pretty. The ham slices, the roast beef, and the other cold cuts should be arranged in overlapping slices on platters; the sliced salmon rolled up and topped with twisted lemon slices; the pâtés topped or surrounded with chopped meat aspic; the caviar set on ice, with little plates of chopped onion, chopped hard-cooked egg yolk and egg white around it; and the salads should be bedded on lettuce. All the foods must be presented decoratively, so that the smorgasbord looks like a colorful painting.

Among the dishes suited to a smorgasbord found elsewhere in this book are *gravad lax*, smoked salmon and scrambled eggs, pickled herring, liver pâté, jellied veal, salmon aspic, crabmeat aspic, lobster, herring salad (this is essential), jellied fruit salad and jellied vegetable salad, all the other vegetable salads such as knob celery salad, cold cauliflower with shrimp, pickled beets, and pickled cucumbers; and among the warm dishes, Janson's temptation, baked anchovies and eggs, ham, creamed potatoes, and Finnish baked mushrooms.

HOW TO MAKE SMØRREBRØD

Unless a book is devoted to nothing else, it is impossible to list the hundreds and hundreds of smørrebrød combinations. I must therefore limit myself to ingredient suggestions and a few words on the actual arrangement of the toppings.

Lettuce, especially the pale green, smooth leaves of the Bibb variety, will set off any food to advantage. Even if you don't want to line the bread of the sandwich with it, use a little at either end, peering out from under the topping.

When a sandwich recipe calls for **mustard,** it is a good idea to sprinkle a little dry mustard powder or to spread prepared mustard thinly and directly on the butter, *under* the topping.

Meat slices should overlap. Ham looks attractive when rolled, and so does salami. (The same applies to salmon.) Slices of ham, salami, other meats, or salmon made into cornucopias, filled with a suitable salad or scrambled eggs, are attractive. Place a parsley spriglet on the filling.

Alternate slices of meat, eggs, tomatoes, or alternate strips of topping look appetizing when chosen with an eye to color, as well as taste, especially when they are placed diagonally across a piece of smørrebrød. They may be topped at right angles with strips of meat, etc.

Asparagus, even one tip only, is a valuable decorative asset. Insert it in a ham or salmon roll, so that the tip is visible. Or contain two or three short asparagus stalks in a ring of red pimiento or green pepper, and lay them on the meat or other toppings.

Pickles are far better looking when cut into strips and placed diagonally on a sandwich.

Grated horseradish and chopped pickles, onions, and eggs (chop the whites and the yolks of the hard-cooked eggs separately), can be arranged in tiny mounds (about ¼ teaspoon) or in strips around, across, or parallel with the topping.

This can also be done with **caviar.** Caviar, naturally, glorifies any smørrebrød. Danish caviar comes from lumpfish, and it is black, small grained, surprisingly good. Danish caviar can be bought in this country, and it is worthwhile to have a jar on hand.

Mushroom caps, sautéed in a little butter but still firm and light, are an excellent sandwich garnish, especially when they are fluted.

One **caper** garnish looks untidy, but three or four, preferably topped with a parsley spriglet, look delightful on an egg and tomato smørrebrød.

Gelée, clear meat aspic, often used on smørrebrød, may be cut either into strips or into small, neat cubes, or coarsely chopped.

Radish roses are decorative and colorful.

Mayonnaise, plain or fancy, looks best when piped through a pastry tube, in strips, swirls, rosettes, etc.

Chives, dill, and **parsley** are essentials for garnish. If no chives are at hand, use the finely chopped green tops of spring onions.

Rings. An onion cut into rings is often used instead of chopped onion because it looks more decorative. But often an onion ring is used to encircle a raw egg yolk, to prevent it from slipping off the sandwich. Also, a salad, such as a herring or Italian salad, is best placed within a raw onion ring to contain it on the sandwich. If an onion ring is unsuitable for the taste of the topping, as in the case of salmon, tomato rings are used instead. The tomato is sliced and the center cut out.

Spriglets and **snippets.** A **spriglet** is the smallest head of an herb or green such as parsley, dill, or watercress. A **snippet** is a tiny piece of a vegetable such as a tomato, with some of the skin on, used mainly to give color.

Springer. A slice of tomato, lemon, cucumber, or beet used as a garnish. A cut is made in the slice, from one side through the center and halfway to the opposite side. By twisting in opposite directions, the slices can be made to stand up on the smørrebrød. Cucumber and lemon springers are often dusted with paprika.

Strips. Smørrebrød arrangements in strips or stripes are common. Minced onion, scrambled egg, caviar, chopped egg, spinach, salads, etc., are often put crosswise or in parallel strips on a sandwich.

Eggs. Raw eggs are part of some sandwiches, such as a beef tartare or a blue cheese smørrebrød. Only the yolk is used, and it is mashed up with the other ingredients before eating. Hard-cooked egg slices, of course, are a very common ingredient or decoration.

New to Americans is the use of scrambled eggs on sandwiches, especially with salmon, a classic combination, or with ham or herring. Danish scrambled eggs are not what we mean by them, but an unsweetened baked custard (*aeggestand*) cut cold into ¾-inch-long strips, which are about 1 inch wide and ½ inch thick. Danish scrambled eggs are fairly tasteless—American scrambled eggs, though not so elegant, have a far better flavor. Also remember that the bread should be firm to stand up under the fillings.

STANDARD SMØRREBRØD
COMBINATIONS

EGG AND TOMATO

Place overlapping slices of hard-cooked egg on one half of buttered rye, crisp, or whole-wheat bread, and overlapping slices of firm tomatoes on the other half. Garnish with watercress.

EGG AND ANCHOVY

Place overlapping slices of hard-cooked egg in two or more rows on buttered rye, crisp, brown, or whole-wheat bread. Place two or three thin fillets of anchovies diagonally across the egg slices. Garnish with radish slices or rosettes.

EGG WITH TOMATO AND HORSERADISH

Similar to egg and anchovy, but substitute strips of grated horseradish for the anchovy and garnish with tomato snippets.

EGG WITH ANCHOVY AND CAPERS

Place anchovy fillets in parallel rows on buttered crisp, brown, or whole-wheat bread. Chop hard-cooked egg and arrange it between the rows of anchovies. Garnish with capers.

EGG AND PICKLES

Arrange rows of overlapping slices of hard-cooked egg on buttered rye, crisp, brown, or whole-wheat bread. Garnish with little mounds of chopped sweet or dill pickles.

EGG WITH CURRY MAYONNAISE AND ANCHOVY

Place slices of hard-cooked egg on rye or crisp bread. Pipe mayonnaise mixed with curry powder over egg slices in strips. Decorate with anchovy snippets. Or use rémoulade sauce, omitting the anchovy.

CHOPPED EGG AND HERRING

Combine chopped egg and any kind of smoked, pickled, or salted chopped herring. Spread on buttered rye, crisp, or brown bread. Top with watercress or parsley spriglets. Or place chopped, boned herrings or herring strips lengthwise on chopped hard-cooked eggs, or overlapping slices of hard-cooked egg.

SMOKED HERRING AND EGG YOLKS

Place strips of smoked herring fillets on buttered rye or brown bread. Leave some space in the middle for an onion ring. Place a raw egg yolk in the onion ring and pile raw onions or chopped radishes at both sides of the yolk.

NOTE: Slide the raw egg yolk on this and on all raw egg yolk sandwiches from a spoon.

ANCHOVIES WITH FRIED OR SCRAMBLED EGG AND CHIVES

Place American-style scrambled egg on buttered rye or whole-wheat bread. Or use a freshly fried egg, sunny side up. Garnish with anchovy fillets placed crosswise on egg, and sprinkle with chives.

SARDINE

Line a slice of buttered rye or whole-wheat bread with a small leaf of Boston lettuce. Cover with small imported sardines packed in tomato sauce. Sprinkle with chopped parsley and garnish with a twist of lemon.

SMOKED SALMON AND SCRAMBLED EGG

Top buttered white bread with smoked salmon slices and, diagonally across the bread, a strip of cold scrambled egg. Decorate with chopped dill.

LOBSTER SALAD

Combine chopped lobster, asparagus tips, and curry or tarragon mayonnaise. Line buttered rye or white bread with lettuce leaves and top with lobster salad. Garnish with additional lobster pieces and asparagus tips.

ROAST BEEF WITH TOMATO AND CUCUMBER

Place one or several slices of cold roast beef on buttered rye, brown, or whole-wheat bread. Garnish with tomato slices and thinly sliced fresh or pickled cucumber.

ROAST BEEF WITH RÉMOULADE SAUCE

Top buttered bread with slices of cold roast beef and stripes of rémoulade sauce (see page 152). Garnish with tomato snippets or twists.

ROAST BEEF WITH HORSERADISH

Top buttered bread with slices of cold roast beef and garnish with grated horseradish. Top with French-fried onions.

ROAST BEEF WITH POTATO SALAD AND CHIVES

Top slices of cold roast beef on buttered bread with a generous mound of well-seasoned potato salad bound with mayonnaise. Sprinkle with chopped chives.

ROAST BEEF AND HAM WITH CHEESE

Place a slice of ham on buttered dark bread and top with parallel strips of rare roast beef, as well as three strips of Camembert cheese placed at right angles on the beef. Sprinkle with paprika.

BRISKET OF CORNED BEEF AND HORSERADISH

Place meat slices on buttered dark bread. Sprinkle with grated horseradish and garnish with pickle strips and a tomato twist.

STEAK AND FRIED EGG

Place strips of cold, juicy steak on buttered bread and top with hot fried egg. Serve immediately.

ROAST LAMB AND CUCUMBER SALAD

Cover lamb slices or strips on buttered bread with drained pickled cucumbers. Garnish with dill, parsley, or tomato.

ROAST PORK AND BEETS

Place slices of cold roast pork on buttered dark bread and garnish with a twist of cooked beet and a little jellied nonfat gravy. Or simply use onion rings or chopped onion and chopped pickles.

TONGUE AND HORSERADISH

Place slices of cold tongue on dark bread buttered with mustard butter (see page 28), or on plainly buttered bread. Sprinkle with grated horseradish in either case.

BACON, ONION, AND APPLES

Place slices of crisp bacon on unbuttered dark bread. Top with crisp-fried onion rings and a slice of fried apple.

BACON AND MUSHROOMS

Top buttered dark bread with crisp-fried bacon slices and sliced fried mushrooms or creamed mushrooms.

HARD-COOKED EGGS AND HERRING SALAD OR DANISH ITALIAN SALAD

Top buttered dark bread with overlapping slices of hard-cooked egg and generous helpings of one or the other salad (see pages 30 and 31).

LIVER PÂTÉ WITH BEETS

Spread dark bread with butter or sliced pork fat and top with a slice of liver pâté (see page 33). Garnish with a strip of cooked beet or chopped meat aspic or a pickle slice.

FRIKADELLER (DANISH MEATBALLS) WITH CUCUMBER SALAD

Place sliced meatballs (see page 111) on buttered bread. Garnish with cucumber salad. Or top meatball slices with aspic strips and shredded red cabbage.

SMOKED EEL

A Danish specialty. Place strips of smoked eel fillet on buttered rye bread and place a little scrambled egg between fish strips.

ROAST CHICKEN

Spread dark or light rye with butter and sprinkle with a little grated horseradish. Top with thin slices of roast chicken. Garnish with liver pâté pushed through a pastry tube and with sliced cucumber.

CHICKEN SALAD

Line a slice of buttered white bread with a lettuce leaf. Top with chicken salad. Garnish with a tiny triangle of pineapple placed in the middle of the chicken salad and green or blue grapes leading from the pineapple to the four corners of the bread.

CAMEMBERT

Spread buttered brown bread with Danish or other Camembert cheese and top with overlapping radish slices.

CUCUMBER BLUE CHEESE

Cut both ends off a small cucumber. Core, taking care not to break the shell. Stuff with an equal mixture of blue cheese and cream or cottage cheese that have been blended together. Chill and cut cucumber into thin slices. Place cucumber slices on buttered dark or white bread. Top with coarsely chopped salted nuts.

HAM AND CHICKEN

Spread toasted white bread with mustard butter (see page 28). Top one half of the bread with minced ham and the other with minced chicken bound with a little heavy cream or mayonnaise. Decorate with watercress.

HAM AND EGG

Mash hard-cooked egg yolks with a little prepared mustard and add a little finely chopped lettuce. Spread on buttered white bread and top with ham cut in strips. Sprinkle with a little grated orange rind.

FESTIVE SMØRREBRØD COMBINATIONS

SHRIMP
Rejer

This is the king of all smørrebrød, a universal favorite eaten in enormous numbers during the fresh-shrimp season. Made with the infinitesimal Danish shrimp, the flavor is good beyond words, but a very acceptable substitute can be made with the canned shrimp imported from Denmark. A minimum of 25 shrimp are placed on buttered white bread, shoulders and tail resting on the butter. A better sandwich is made from 50, 60, or more shrimp, layered or arranged in a pyramid. Serve with lemon twists and freshly ground black pepper.

BEEF TARTARE

Butter a slice of dark or light rye bread and cover with a large spoonful of freshly ground (or, better still, freshly scraped) sirloin or tenderloin, *which must be raw*. Make a well in the center of the beef and place an onion ring on it. Slip an egg yolk into the onion ring. Garnish with mounds or strips of grated horseradish, grated onion, anchovy fillets, and capers.

SMOKED SALMON WITH SPINACH AND MUSHROOM CAPS

Place overlapping slices of smoked salmon on buttered dark bread. Top with a diagonal strip of warm creamed spinach. Place several broiled mushroom caps on spinach. Or substitute asparagus tips for spinach.

HAM AND CHICKEN SALAD

Place cornucopias of ham filled with chicken salad on buttered white bread. Garnish with parsley or dill sprigs.

GOOSE LIVER PÂTÉ WITH HAM AND MADEIRA

Place thinly sliced ham on buttered dark or white bread. Top with spoonfuls of goose liver pâté. Sprinkle with chopped Madeira aspic (a clear meat aspic to which a little Madeira has been added for flavoring) and garnish with watercress.

BLUE CHEESE AND EGGS

Spread blue cheese on buttered white bread, making a well in center of cheese. Place an egg yolk in well. Decorate with radish rosettes or slices. When eating the sandwich, break yolk and spread it evenly across cheese.

FRIED FISH FILLETS WITH RÉMOULADE SAUCE
In Denmark plaice is used for this sandwich, but it can be made with sole or other filleted white fish. Season a 4-inch-square piece of fish fillet with salt and pepper. Dip into 2 tablespoons milk, then into 2 tablespoons dry bread crumbs. Melt 2 tablespoons butter and fry fish in it on both sides. Place warm fish on buttered or unbuttered white bread, and top with 2 tablespoons rémoulade sauce (see page 152). Or place fish on plate and serve bread separately.

HANS CHRISTIAN ANDERSEN'S SANDWICH
(I won't swear to the authenticity, but I will swear to the taste.) Butter 1 slice white bread with 1 tablespoon butter. Place 2 slices of crisply fried bacon on top. Top with 4 paper-thin slices of firm tomato and 2 thin slices of liver pâté (see page 33). Garnish with 2 or 3 cubes of meat aspic and 1 teaspoon grated horseradish.

LIVER PÂTÉ AND TONGUE
Butter 1 slice white or dark bread with 1 tablespoon butter. Place 2 finger-length slices of liver pâté (see page 33) on 2 slices of tongue or boiled ham and roll. Top bread with meat rolls and garnish with sliced or chopped sweet or dill pickles and parsley sprigs.

THE VET'S MIDNIGHT SUPPER
Spread 1 slice dark or light rye bread with 2 tablespoons pork drippings or meat jelly. Top with 2 slices of liver pâté (see page 33), chopped meat aspic, and thin slices of cold spiced breast of veal (see page 32). Decorate with watercress.

LOBSTER

Blend about ½ cup cold chopped lobster with 2 tablespoons heavy cream and season with salt and pepper to taste. Spread 1 slice of white bread with 1 tablespoon butter. Top with creamed lobster. Place about 2 tablespoons cold chopped lobster in a cup made with 1 Bibb lettuce leaf and set this on creamed lobster. Serve with lemon twists.

SCRAMBLED EGG WITH MUSSELS AND SPINACH

Beat 1 egg with 2 teaspoons water and 1 tablespoon melted butter. Cook over low heat, stirring until scrambled. Place 6 well-scrubbed mussels in a pan. Shake over low heat until mussels open. Remove mussels from shells. Steam ½ cup fresh, finely chopped spinach until tender, about 2 to 3 minutes. Drain thoroughly. Spread 2 slices of bread with 2 tablespoons butter. Place strips of scrambled egg, spinach, and rows of mussels diagonally across the bread.

MEAT SALAD

Combine ¼ cup finely chopped cold beef, veal, or pork with 2 tablespoons plain or flavored mayonnaise. Spread on buttered dark bread and sprinkle with chopped onion, diced cucumber, or pickles.

COD OR SHAD ROE SALAD

Cover roe with boiling salted water. Simmer over low heat for 30 to 40 minutes or until firm. Remove skin. Press roe through a sieve. Season with salt and pepper to taste. Stir in 1 tablespoon lemon juice and ½ teaspoon curry powder. Spread on slices of dark or white bread that have been buttered with 1 tablespoon butter each. Garnish with watercress and lemon twists. This will serve 2 or 3, depending on size of roe.

* * *

Make your own combinations, provided they are judiciously matched to each other, as to both flavor and texture. Remember, too, that the bread used should complement the toppings.

HOW TO EAT SMØRREBRØD

Obviously, the more elaborate forms of smørrebrød are eaten sitting down, and using a knife and fork. The simpler and simplest form of smørrebrød can also be eaten out of hand; you are the judge of how to eat an open-faced sandwich without dripping or scattering its parts all over you. However, the general custom is to eat a good open-faced sandwich or smørrebrød at mealtimes by sitting down and using a knife and fork and not one's hands. In other words, a proper smørrebrød can't be eaten on the run like so many American sandwiches.

FATS, FLAVORED BUTTERS, AND MAYONNAISE USED FOR SPREADING ON SMØRREBRØD

DUCK OR GOOSE DRIPPINGS

The flavor of both of these is excellent, but both have a tendency to be too liquid to be spread on bread. To remedy this, blend a little melted lard into the drippings—just enough to achieve proper spreading consistency. Chill before using. If stored in a covered container in the refrigerator, these will keep for a week or so.

LEMON BUTTER

Cream ½ cup softened butter. Gradually stir in 2 tablespoons lemon juice and, if desired, 2 tablespoons finely chopped parsley or dill.

CURRY BUTTER

Cream ½ cup softened butter. Stir in ½ teaspoon curry powder and a little black pepper or a dash of hot pepper sauce.

MUSTARD BUTTER

Cream ½ cup softened butter. Stir in 1 teaspoon or more prepared mustard, or ¼ to ½ teaspoon dry mustard.

ANCHOVY BUTTER

Cream ½ cup softened butter. Stir in anchovy paste to taste, starting with ¼ teaspoon.

TOMATO MAYONNAISE

Add 2 teaspoons tomato purée to 1 cup mayonnaise.

CUCUMBER MAYONNAISE

Add ½ cup finely chopped cucumber and 1 teaspoon chopped parsley to 1 cup mayonnaise. Good for fish sandwiches.

HORSERADISH MAYONNAISE

Add a little grated horseradish to taste to mayonnaise.

NOTE: Both butters and mayonnaise may be flavored in any desired way, to suit personal tastes and the topping that will be used in a sandwich. Instant onion and garlic powders, dried herbs, bottled sauces, and spices, all lend themselves as flavorings.

MORE SMØRREBRØD AND SMORGASBORD DISHES

Blue Cheese Spread

ABOUT 2¼ CUPS SPREAD

Make it with any kind of blue cheese.

1 ½ cups blue cheese
¾ cup sweet butter, softened
2 teaspoons grated onion

Dash of hot pepper sauce
1 cup finely chopped blanched salted almonds

Mash blue cheese with a fork until smooth. Beat in butter, grated onion, and hot pepper sauce. Blend thoroughly. Form into a ball and roll in chopped almonds. Chill before serving. Or make individual servings by shaping cheese mixture into tiny balls and rolling in chopped almonds.

Herring Salad

Sildesalat

4 TO 6 SERVINGS

Herring salad is a favorite throughout Scandinavia, and though the basic ingredients remain the same, each cook adjusts the quantities of each to personal taste. Personally, I like a salad that does not taste too powerfully of herring.

Danish cooks make a "fine" herring salad by omitting the cream or white sauce dressing and chopping all the ingredients on a chopping board until they form a soft mixture. This is good for spreading on smørrebrød, but a diced salad (as below) with some body to it tastes better, to my mind. If you like, add 1 cup any cooked chopped meat to salad.

1 salt herring, filleted, or one 5-ounce jar herring, or more, drained
1 cup diced cold boiled potato
1 cup diced pickled beets
½ cup diced peeled apple
⅓ cup diced onion
1 teaspoon mustard
1 teaspoon sugar

1 tablespoon vinegar
1 cup thick white sauce, cold, or ⅔ cup heavy cream, whipped
Salt
Pepper
Chopped parsley
Hard-cooked egg slices

Soak salt herring overnight in cold water; drain and dice. Combine all ingredients, blending in white sauce or cream last, and season with salt and pepper. Decorate with chopped parsley and slices of hard-cooked eggs. Chill before using.

NOTE: The dressing should barely hold the salad together.

Danish Italian Salad

Italiensk Salad

4 TO 6 SERVINGS

---

1 cup diced cooked carrots
1 cup finely cut cooked
asparagus
1 cup cooked small
green peas
½ cup mayonnaise,
or to taste

Tarragon vinegar or
juice of up to 1
lemon
¼ teaspoon dry
mustard, or to taste

Combine carrots, asparagus, and peas. Thin mayonnaise with a little tarragon vinegar or lemon juice and stir in a little dry mustard. Toss vegetables in mayonnaise and chill. If this salad is to be used on smørrebrød, be sure to place a lettuce leaf on the buttered bread before topping it with the salad. The lettuce will prevent the bread from becoming soggy.

Variation
Add either or both ½ cup cooked elbow
macaroni and 1 cup ham or tongue cut
into julienne strips.

Danish Chicken Salad

Hønsesalat

4 TO 6 SERVINGS

---

2 cups diced cooked white
  chicken meat
1 cup knob celery cut in
  julienne strips, or
  chopped celery
1 cup heavy cream

½ teaspoon mild mustard,
  or to taste
Salt
Pepper
Lettuce
Capers
Tomato twists

Combine chicken and knob celery. Whip cream until slightly stiffened. Stir in mustard and salt and pepper to taste. Fold chicken mixture into cream. Pile on lettuce leaves and decorate with capers and tomato twists.

Spiced Breast of Veal

Rullepølse

4 TO 6 SERVINGS

This recipe, the best I know for the dish, comes from Craig Claiborne, the distinguished food editor of *The New York Times*, who is an accomplished chef. The sliced meat may be used for smørrebrød, but it is also delicious for a cold buffet.

1 breast of veal
1 pound fatback, sliced
1 tablespoon pepper
Salt
1 tablespoon plus ¼
  teaspoon saltpeter

1 tablespoon ground
  allspice
1 cup chopped onion
5 tablespoons finely
  chopped dill or
  parsley

Have the butcher bone the breast of veal and flatten it. Trim it to make a large square. Arrange the fatback on the veal and sprinkle with pepper, 1 tablespoon salt, 1 tablespoon saltpeter, allspice, onion, and dill or parsley. Roll the veal jelly-roll fashion, wrap the meat roll in a clean white cloth, and tie tightly with string. Place enough cold water in a crock to cover the rolled veal. Dissolve enough salt in the water so that a medium-size potato will float in the brine. Stir in ¼ teaspoon saltpeter. Place the veal in brine bath. Weigh it down with a heavy plate or other weight and let it rest in a cool place for 5 or 6 days. Drain the veal. Place it in a large kettle and cover with water. Add salt to taste and bring to a boil. Simmer, covered, 1½ hours. Remove from cooking liquid and weigh down once more. Refrigerate at least 24 hours. Remove the cloth. Cut into wafer-thin slices.

Liver Pâté

Leverpostej

4 TO 6 SERVINGS

Liver pâté is a regular part of the Danish diet, and there are as many recipes for it as there are Danish cooks. Generally the pâté is not like the densely textured French pâté, but more along the lines of a very firm soufflé.

2 pounds pork or calf's liver

1 medium-size onion

1 pound pork fat

3 tablespoons butter or margarine

3 tablespoons flour

2 cups half-and-half

2 eggs, well beaten

2 teaspoons anchovy paste, or to taste

1 teaspoon salt

1 teaspoon pepper

½ teaspoon ground ginger

Set oven at 325°.

In a food processor or blender, or with the finest blade of the meat grinder, grind liver and onion twice. Grind pork fat twice. Melt butter and stir in flour. Gradually stir in half-and-half, then cook over low heat, stirring constantly, until thickened and smooth. Add ground pork fat and stir until fat has melted. Remove from heat. Add liver and all other ingredients and blend thoroughly. Spoon into 2-quart baking dish. Place dish in baking pan containing hot water. Bake for 1½ to 2 hours, or until pâté tests done. Cover with lid or aluminum foil if top is browning too quickly. Replenish water in baking pan if necessary. Cool, scraping off fat before serving on smørrebrød or the cold table.

Danish Lobster or Shrimp Patties

Hummer eller Reje Postej

4 TO 6 SERVINGS

4 tablespoons butter
1 ½ tablespoons flour
1 cup milk
⅓ cup heavy cream
2 egg yolks, well beaten
2 tablespoons Cognac
½ teaspoon dry mustard
Salt
Cayenne

1 cup diced boiled
lobster meat or 1
cup chopped
cooked, shelled
shrimp
½ pound mushrooms,
sliced
Patty shells, heated

Melt 2 tablespoons butter in top of double boiler over very low heat. Stir in flour and cook over very low heat about 3 minutes, stirring constantly. Gradually stir in milk and cook over very low heat until smooth and thickened, stirring all the time. Place top of double boiler over lower portion, filled with simmering water. Cook sauce about 15 minutes, stirring occasionally (practically all white sauces are undercooked and taste raw). Remove sauce from bottom of double boiler and place over direct heat. Cook it down to three-fourths of its volume, stirring constantly. Remove from heat and stir in cream. Beat together egg yolks, Cognac, and dry mustard. Beat mixture into hot sauce, a little at a time. Season with salt and a little cayenne to taste. Add lobster or shrimp to sauce and cook for about 3 minutes over boiling water. Cook mushrooms in 2 tablespoons hot butter until softened but still firm and white. Add to lobster or shrimp mixture. Spoon into patty shells and serve immediately.

> NOTE: The mixture may also be served in tartlet shells. If these are very small, omit sautéed mushrooms, but garnish with a sliver of raw mushroom sprinkled with a little lemon juice to keep it white.

Filled Cheese Puffs

Vandbakkelsedejg med Fyld

ABOUT 12 MEDIUM-SIZE PUFFS

1 cup water
¼ cup butter
1 cup sifted flour
3 eggs, at room
  temperature

¼ cup grated
  Parmesan or
  other cheese
½ teaspoon salt
⅛ teaspoon pepper
Ham Filling (recipe
  below)

Set oven at 400°.

Combine water and butter in a saucepan and bring to a boil. Remove from heat. Add flour all at once. Beat until glossy over low heat, until dough does not cling to the sides of the pan any longer. Remove from heat; do not overcook, or puffs won't rise in baking. Beat in eggs, one at a time. Beat in cheese, salt, and pepper. Shape with pastry bag or spoon on ungreased baking sheet. Place puffs about 2 inches apart to allow spreading. Bake for 10 minutes. Reduce heat to 350° and bake 20 to 25 minutes longer. Do not remove puffs from oven until quite firm to the touch. Prick the side of the puffs with a fork. Replace in oven for 5 minutes to allow puffs to dry. Cool away from drafts before filling. For filling, cut puffs horizontally with a sharp knife. Fill with creamed eggs, chicken, seafood, ham, or a heavy cheese sauce.

Ham Filling for Tartlets

ABOUT 2½ CUPS

½ cup finely chopped
shallots
2 tablespoons butter
2 cups shredded ham or
canned loin of pork
or Canadian bacon

⅔ cup sour cream
2 egg yolks
¼ cup finely chopped
parsley or dill
Dash of hot pepper
sauce

Cook shallots in hot butter until soft and golden. Add meat and cook over low heat about 5 minutes, or until thoroughly heated through. Stir constantly. Beat sour cream with egg yolks, parsley or dill, and hot pepper sauce. Add to meat mixture and cook until just heated. Do not boil. Use as a filling for tiny tartlets, patties, or cheese puffs, or spread on hot toast.

Scandinavian Pickled Beets

4 TO 6 SERVINGS

They are served everywhere, constantly.

24 medium-size beets
1 cup sugar
3 cups white vinegar
2 bay leaves

1 piece of fresh
horseradish
(optional)

Scrub beets thoroughly and cook in boiling salt water until tender. Meanwhile, boil together sugar, vinegar, and bay leaves. Peel cooked beets by slipping skins off while still warm. Slice— this is optional. Place beets in boiling vinegar mixture. Bring to a boil. Boil 1 minute. Place in sterilized jars. A small piece of fresh horseradish in each jar will help preserve and flavor beets.

Pickled Cucumbers

4 TO 6 SERVINGS

As common throughout Scandinavia as coleslaw is in America.

½ cup white vinegar
2 tablespoons water
¼ teaspoon salt
⅛ teaspoon white pepper
3 tablespoons sugar

3 tablespoons minced
dill or parsley
2 medium-size
cucumbers

Combine all ingredients except cucumbers. Wash and dry cucumbers. Do not peel. Slice crosswise as thinly as possible—

the cucumbers should be almost transparent. Place in serving dish. Pour dressing over cucumbers and refrigerate 3 hours or more before serving.

NOTE: Although it is not the Scandinavian way, I find it better to drain the cucumbers before serving.

Swedish Horseradish Beet Salad

4 TO 6 SERVINGS

I had this on a Swedish train, where it was very suitably served with fried fish.

½ cup sour cream or
plain yogurt, or ¼
cup sour cream plus
¼ cup yogurt
3 tablespoons freshly
grated horseradish
½ teaspoon sugar
½ teaspoon salt

⅛ teaspoon white
pepper
3 to 4 cups cooked
beets, cut in
julienne strips
Lettuce
Parsley sprigs

Blend together first five ingredients and combine with beets. Chill; serve on lettuce. Decorate with sprigs of parsley.

Danish Knob Celery Salad

4 TO 6 SERVINGS

Knob celery is a biggish dark brown root that must be peeled. It tastes like celery, but much more so, and is a great favorite throughout Europe.

3 medium-size celery knobs
⅓ cup heavy cream,
  whipped
⅓ cup mayonnaise

1 teaspoon prepared
  mustard
Lettuce

Peel celery knobs until only white part shows. Cut into slices about ¹⁄₁₆ inch thick or as thin as you can make them. Cut slices into slivers the size of toothpicks. Combine whipped cream, mayonnaise, and mustard. Fold in celery slivers. Chill for 2 hours or longer. Serve on a bed of lettuce.

NOTE: This salad is a standard item in Denmark, where it goes not only to the cold table and sandwiches, but is also served as a relish with meats and fish.

Sour Cream Cucumber Salad

4 TO 6 SERVINGS

4 large cucumbers
1 tablespoon salt
⅔ cup sour cream or
  plain yogurt
1 ½ tablespoons white
  vinegar

2 tablespoons salad
  oil
½ teaspoon sugar
3 tablespoons
  minced dill
Salt
Pepper

Scrub cucumbers but do not peel. Cut off ends. Score with tines of a fork. Slice crosswise thinly. Sprinkle with salt and let stand at room temperature for 1 hour. Drain and rinse to remove salt. Squeeze dry. Combine sour cream, vinegar, salad oil, sugar, and dill. Pour over cucumbers. Add salt and pepper to taste. Chill before serving.

NOTE: To be authentic, these cucumbers should be served in a glass dish and decorated with dill sprigs.

Jellied Pineapple and Cherry Salad
4 TO 6 SERVINGS

For the smorgasbord or as a dessert.

Two 3-ounce packages
lemon-flavored
gelatin
1 teaspoon salt
2 cups boiling water
2 cups cold water
2 tablespoons lemon
juice

1 cup drained canned
pineapple tidbits
2 cups (two 8-ounce
cans) drained
cherries, pitted
and halved
Crisp salad greens

Dissolve gelatin and salt in boiling water. Add cold water and lemon juice. Chill until slightly thickened. Fold in pineapple and cherries. Pour into 2-quart mold rinsed with cold water. Chill until firm. Unmold on crisp salad greens.

Janson's Temptation
ABOUT 10 SMORGASBORD SERVINGS OR
4 TO 6 MAIN-COURSE SERVINGS

An immensely popular Swedish combination of anchovies and potatoes, two foods of which the Swedes are very fond indeed. As for the unknown Janson, who knows whether he fell?

6 medium-size potatoes,
peeled and sliced
wafer thin
12 anchovy fillets,
drained, cut in pieces

1 onion, diced fine
¼ teaspoon pepper
2 cups light cream
2 tablespoons butter

Set oven at 350°.

Place a layer of half of the potatoes in a buttered baking dish. Top with anchovies and onion. Sprinkle with pepper and top with remaining potatoes. Pour cream over mixture and dot with butter. Bake about 30 minutes or until potatoes are tender and the top delicately browned.

Baked Anchovies and Eggs

A favorite hot smorgasbord combination. If you like a stronger anchovy flavor, increase the quantity of anchovies according to taste.

8 anchovy fillets, drained	2 cups light cream
3 eggs	2 tablespoons chopped parsley

Set oven at 350°.

Place anchovies in a buttered baking dish. Beat together eggs, cream, and parsley. Pour over anchovies. Bake about 25 minutes or until set and golden brown. Serve hot on the smorgasbord table.

Oat Cakes

½ cup butter	2 cups instant oatmeal
½ cup sugar	

Melt butter and stir in sugar. Add oatmeal. Cook over medium heat until oatmeal is golden brown. Moisten egg cups, small individual baking dishes, or tea-sized muffin pans with cold water and pack firmly with oatmeal mixture. Chill. Unmold and serve with hot buttermilk soup (see page 51).

NOTE: In Denmark the cakes are split and the soup poured over them.

Danish Bacon and Egg Pancake

Flaeskeaeggekage

A very pleasant luncheon or supper dish. The tastier the bacon, the better the pancake.

*½ pound sliced Danish
    or other bacon
6 eggs
½ cup milk or light
    cream*

*1 tablespoon flour
½ teaspoon salt
3 tablespoons
    chopped chives*

Fry bacon in a skillet until golden brown. Remove bacon and drain. Keep fat in skillet. Crumble bacon into small pieces. Beat eggs with milk, flour, salt, and chives. Reheat bacon fat, and pour egg mixture into it. When omelet begins to set, sprinkle the crumbled bacon on top. Lift cooked omelet edges with a fork so that the uncooked portion runs underneath. Cook until eggs are set and golden brown. Fold and serve hot. For a firm omelet, turn on a plate and replace omelet in skillet uncooked side down. Brown lightly and serve.

Finnish Spinach Pancakes

Finland, like Sweden, is a pancake land. These spinach pancakes, which make a good entrée, should be made small and thin, since, thanks to the spinach, they take longer to cook through than plain pancakes.

1 cup milk
1 teaspoon salt
⅛ teaspoon grated nutmeg
1 cup flour
2 tablespoons melted
  butter
2 eggs
1 teaspoon sugar

½ pound fresh
  spinach, blanched
  and chopped, or 1
  package frozen
  chopped spinach,
  thawed and drained
Butter

Season milk with salt and nutmeg. Sift in flour, a little at a time, beating constantly. Stir in melted butter. Let mixture stand for 30 minutes to 1 hour. Beat eggs with sugar and stir into batter. Add spinach. Prepare pancakes as usual. Cook pancakes in buttered pan. In Finland, these pancakes are served with lingonberries.

Swedish Pancakes

Plättar

To be authentically small and very thin, Swedish pancakes ought to be baked in a Swedish pancake pan, which has depressions for each pancake. They can be bought in good housewares stores or in Scandinavian supply houses. But these pancakes may also be baked on a hot griddle, by the tablespoonfuls.

Incidentally, pancakes are a staple in all Scandinavian countries, and basically, there is not a great deal of difference among them. The Norwegians often eat theirs cold, folded over.

4 eggs, separated	3 tablespoons sour
1 cup flour	cream
½ teaspoon salt	Butter
1 teaspoon sugar	Lingonberry
1 cup milk	preserves or
	applesauce

Beat egg yolks until thick. Sift together flour, salt, and sugar. Add to egg yolks alternately with milk. Stir in sour cream. Beat egg whites until stiff but not dry. Fold into batter. Heat pancake pan and butter each depression. Pour about a tablespoon of batter into each depression and spread out evenly. Brown on one side, turn, and brown on the other side. Serve at once with preserves or applesauce.

SOUPS
AND
DUMPLINGS

Of all the Scandinavian countries, Denmark, I think, is the home of the most appealing soups. There, in a country that is really part of the northern continental European tradition, where soup is often the meal or at least the filler that saves on more costly main dishes, I find Scandinavia's most interesting soups. But I do not think that Scandinavians as a whole go in for soups—with the exception of *gule aerter*, yellow pea soup—in the way the Italians and French do, where nature's climate and its bounties made a great variety of soups possible. Gruels and porridges, as in Germany, used to be the national diet of the poor in Scandinavia. To alleviate the monotony of cereal gruels, small dumplings were used to fortify the soups. Big, and at times even stuffed, dumplings served to make a more substantial meal. Since dumpling recipes are far more typical of Germanic cooking, I shall quote just two of them I thought typical of Scandinavian tradition, or, at least, as more interesting to make and to eat. And remember, you will not find here the refined little quenelles and other delicate tiny dumplings of fine French cooking.

Yellow Pea Soup

Gule Aerter

6 SERVINGS

An all-Scandinavian favorite and a meal in itself. In Denmark, the soup and the meats are served separately, with pickled beets, a good sharp mustard, dark rye bread and butter, and ice-cold *snaps* and beer. The Danes start with a plate of soup, and eat the second plate alternately with the meats and fixings.

1 ½ cups yellow split peas
1 quart water
1 teaspoon salt
1 pound streaky bacon or salt pork in one piece
1 peeled and diced celery knob or 1 cup chopped celery
3 sliced leeks or 1 cup green onion tops
6 cups water
3 sliced carrots

3 medium-size potatoes, peeled and diced
1 large onion, chopped
1 pound Canadian bacon, cut into ¼-inch slices
One 4-ounce can Danish or other Vienna sausages, drained

Combine split peas, water, and salt. Bring to a boil and simmer until tender and very soft—about 1½ to 2 hours. Skim off pea skins as they float to the top. Force through a sieve or a food mill or purée in blender. Place bacon or salt pork in a large saucepan. (If salt pork is very salty, soak in cold water for 30 minutes to 1 hour before using.) Add celery knob and leeks or green onion tops. Add water. Cover and simmer for 1½ to 2 hours or until meat is tender. Add carrots, potatoes, and onion.

Cover and simmer until vegetables are tender. Remove bacon or salt pork. Cut into slices. Skim fat from broth or chill in refrigerator, remove fat, and reheat. Stir pea purée into broth. If necessary, add additional water until soup has the consistency of thick cream. Add sliced Canadian bacon and Vienna sausages cut into ½-inch pieces. Heat soup to the boiling point. Simmer 5 minutes. Remove Canadian bacon and serve slices with the slices of bacon or salt pork. Serve soup separately.

Mushroom Soup with Madeira

Kalvesuppe med Madeira og Champignons

6 SERVINGS

⅓ cup water
⅛ teaspoon salt
½ tablespoon lemon
    juice
3 tablespoons butter
¼ pound very white
    mushrooms
2 tablespoons flour

6 to 8 cups hot chicken
    stock, depending
    on how thick a
    soup you want
Salt
White pepper
⅓ cup Madeira or
    more, to taste

Bring water, salt, lemon juice, and 1 tablespoon butter to a boil in an enamel saucepan. (A metal saucepan will darken mushrooms, which must remain very white.) Trim and wash mushrooms; slice thin. Add mushrooms to liquid and stir to cover them with the liquid. Simmer, covered, for 5 minutes, stirring or tossing frequently. In deep kettle, melt 2 tablespoons butter and stir in flour. Gradually add hot stock, stirring constantly. Simmer, covered, for 10 minutes, stirring frequently. Season with salt and pepper to taste. Add mushrooms and mushroom liquor and heat through. Just before serving, remove from heat and stir in Madeira.

> NOTE: For a richer soup, stir ⅓ to ½ cup heavy cream into soup before adding Madeira.

Scandinavian Brown Cabbage Soup

4 TO 6 SERVINGS

This soup is served in all of Scandinavia. In Sweden, more sugar is used, because the Swedes use far more sugar in their food than the other Nordics.

1 large head cabbage, cored and shredded
¼ cup butter
2 tablespoons brown sugar

1 quart bouillon or more, depending on thickness of soup desired
1 teaspoon salt
½ teaspoon pepper
¼ teaspoon ground allspice

In a deep kettle brown cabbage on all sides in hot butter. The color should be a light brown. Stir occasionally. Add sugar and cook until sugar is completely dissolved, stirring constantly. Add bouillon, salt, pepper, and allspice and simmer covered, about 1 hour. Serve with dumplings.

Norwegian Cauliflower Soup

Blomkålsuppe

4 TO 6 SERVINGS

One of Norway's national soups. Unlike most cream soups, it is not very thick.

1 large or 2 medium-size cauliflowers	2 tablespoons flour
1 ½ to 1 ¾ quarts boiling water	2 egg yolks
1 tablespoon salt	2 tablespoons heavy cream
1 ½ tablespoons butter	⅛ teaspoon grated nutmeg (optional)

Trim cauliflower and break into buds, but keep stalks and trimmings. Place all cauliflower parts into boiling water and add salt. Simmer until buds are just tender. Remove buds and keep hot. Continue simmering until stalks and trimmings are very soft and mushy. Strain and reserve stock. Melt butter and stir in flour. When blended and smooth, add hot stock, a little at a time, stirring constantly. Cover and simmer 10 to 15 minutes, stirring occasionally. Beat egg yolks with heavy cream and nutmeg. Remove soup from heat. Beat one cupful of hot soup into the egg-cream mixture, one tablespoon at a time. Gradually stir in remaining soup. Return soup to lowest possible heat and heat through. Do not boil, or even simmer, or soup will curdle. Add hot cauliflower buds and serve immediately.

Norwegian Spinach Soup

Spinatsuppe

4 TO 6 SERVINGS

Another favorite Norwegian soup.

2 pounds spinach, chopped, or 2 packages frozen chopped spinach	2 tablespoons flour
	Salt
	Pepper
1 ½ quarts hot beef bouillon	2 hard-cooked eggs, sliced
2 tablespoons butter	

Cook spinach in hot bouillon for 10 minutes. Drain, reserving liquid. Keep spinach hot. Melt butter and stir in flour. When blended and smooth add hot stock, a little at a time, stirring constantly. Cover and simmer 5 minutes, stirring occasionally. Add spinach, salt, and pepper, blending thoroughly. Cover and simmer 5 minutes longer, stirring occasionally. Serve with hard-cooked egg slices floating on top.

Finnish Summer Vegetable Soup

Kesäkeitto

4 TO 6 SERVINGS

Good for a summer luncheon, followed by pie or cake. The flavor of this soup depends on the freshness of the vegetables, which should be cut into small pieces.

1 quart water
1 tablespoon salt
1 cup French-style green
   beans
1 cup sliced carrots
1 cup cubed peeled
   potatoes
1 cup fresh peas
1 cup cauliflower
   buds

½ cup chopped
   spinach
2 to 3 tablespoons
   flour, depending
   on thickness of
   soup desired
1 quart milk
2 tablespoons butter
¼ cup chopped
   parsley

Bring water and salt to a boil in deep kettle. Add green beans, carrots, and potatoes. When these are half cooked, add peas, cauliflower, and spinach. Cook until vegetables are just tender; do not overcook. Mix flour with a little of the cold milk to a smooth paste. Stir into hot soup. Add remaining milk and simmer soup for 10 minutes. Remove from heat and stir in butter and parsley.

Danish Hot Buttermilk Soup

Kaernemaelsuppe

4 TO 6 SERVINGS

Think of it as a dessert rather than a soup, and you'll like it after a heavy main dish.

½ cup raw rice
2 quarts buttermilk
Grated rind of 1 lemon
1 cinnamon stick
⅓ cup raisins

2 egg yolks
1 tablespoon sugar
Chopped almonds
Whipped cream

Crush rice with meat pounder or hammer to the consistency of coarse salt. (This is best done by placing the rice in a heavy paper bag or wrapping it in a kitchen towel.) Combine rice and buttermilk. Add lemon rind, cinnamon, and raisins. Cook over low heat, stirring constantly, until thickened. (The constant stirring is needed to prevent the soup from curdling.) Beat the egg yolks with the sugar in a tureen. Gradually beat in the hot soup. Serve with chopped almonds and cold whipped cream.

NOTE: This soup may also be served slightly chilled.

Cherry Soup

Kirsebaersuppe

4 TO 6 SERVINGS

Serve it hot as a soup or cold as a dessert.

2 pounds sweet cherries	1/4 cup water
2 quarts water	Juice of 1 lemon
1/3 cup sugar, or to taste	1/3 cup Peter Heering
1 cinnamon stick	cordial (optional)
Grated rind of 1 lemon	Whipped cream
2 tablespoons cornstarch	(optional)

Pit cherries and save juice. Reserve 1 cup pitted cherries. Cook remaining cherries and juice in water, with sugar, cinnamon stick, and lemon rind until soft. Remove cinnamon stick. Force through strainer or food mill or purée in blender. Mix cornstarch with 1/4 cup water to a smooth paste. Stir into soup. Cook 5 minutes or until smooth and thickened, stirring constantly. Stir in lemon juice, Peter Heering, and reserved cherries. If served as a dessert, top each helping with a spoonful of whipped cream. Serve with small almond macaroons.

Apple Soup

Aeblesuppe

6 SERVINGS

The soup should have the consistency of heavy cream.

1 ½ pounds tart apples, preferably greenings
2 ½ quarts water
1 cinnamon stick
Rind of 1 lemon, cut into strips
¼ cup cornstarch
½ cup water
¼ cup sugar
½ cup white wine
6 pieces zwieback or rusks
Whipped cream

Quarter and core apples. Do not peel. Place apples in deep kettle and add 1 ½ quarts of the water, cinnamon stick, and lemon rind. Cook over low heat until apples are very soft. Do not drain apples. Remove cinnamon stick. Force apples through a strainer or a food mill or purée in blender. Add remaining quart of water. Blend cornstarch in ½ cup water to a smooth paste. Stir into soup. Cook soup over low heat until thickened and smooth, stirring constantly. Add sugar and white wine. The soup should be tart but, if desired, add more sugar. Crush zwieback and distribute in 6 soup plates. Ladle soup over crumbs. Serve hot or cold with whipped cream.

Beer Soup

Øllebrød

4 TO 6 SERVINGS

This is a very old and very popular Danish dish, not a soup in our sense of the word, but a thick pottage. Unfortunately, it is seldom served to foreigners. The proper ingredients are a sweet, dark nonalcoholic malt beer sometimes found in German and Scandinavian neighborhoods and dark Danish rye bread. In lieu of the Danish *hvidtøl* a dark ale may be used, and dark pumpernickel can be substituted for the bread. But the taste will not be the same.

8 slices pumpernickel	Sugar
2 to 3 cups dark ale	Heavy cream, plain
1 cup water	or whipped
Grated rind and juice	
of 1 lemon	

Break bread into small pieces. Place in deep dish. Combine ale and water and pour over bread. Soak at least 3 hours or overnight. Simmer over low heat until soup thickens to desired consistency. Force through strainer or purée in blender. Stir in lemon rind and juice. Sweeten to taste. Bring once more to a boil. Serve hot with plain or whipped cream.

Chervil Soup

4 TO 6 SERVINGS

This soup can be found throughout Scandinavia. A spring and summer soup.

¼ cup butter
¼ cup flour
6 to 8 cups hot bouillon,
  depending on how
  thick a soup you want
Salt

Pepper
2 boiled carrots, sliced
⅓ cup minced fresh
  chervil
Poached eggs

Melt butter and stir in flour. Cook 2 minutes over medium heat, stirring constantly. Do not brown. Gradually stir in hot bouillon. Season with salt and pepper to taste. Simmer, covered, over low heat 15 minutes, stirring occasionally. Add sliced carrots and heat through. Just before serving, add chervil. Do not boil soup, or chervil will loose its delicate taste and fresh green color. Serve with poached eggs; place 1 poached egg in each soup plate and ladle soup carefully over it.

Swedish Potato Dumplings

The Swedes like dumplings, and eat them not only in soup but by themselves, served with butter or a sauce.

¼ cup butter
2 egg yolks
½ cup fine dry
  bread crumbs
½ cup firmly packed
  cooked mashed
  potatoes

¼ teaspoon salt
1 cup ham or
  luncheon meat, cut
  into ½-inch cubes

Cream butter and beat in egg yolks. Stir in bread crumbs, potatoes, and salt. Mix thoroughly. Knead and shape into a long roll.

Cut off pieces about the size of a walnut. Flatten each piece in the hand and place a cube of ham in middle. Shape into a round dumpling enclosing ham completely. Cook, uncovered, in simmering soup or simmering water 10 minutes. Cover and cook 5 minutes longer.

Swedish Meat Dumplings for Soup

¼ cup ground beef
¼ cup ground pork
1 small onion, ground
½ teaspoon salt

¼ teaspoon pepper
⅛ teaspoon ground allspice
2 tablespoons flour

Combine all ingredients except flour and blend thoroughly. Shape into small balls the size of a large marble. Roll in flour. Drop into simmering soup and simmer 20 minutes.

FISH

_A_ ll Scandinavians love fish. Until recently fish has been the
staple diet of Norway, whose fisheries supplied herring and cod
to Europe, if not to the world, since the Middle Ages. Cod and
herring are simple fish, and typical bounty from Norway's un-
believably beautiful coast. To this day, there is nothing finer
than freshly and plainly cooked Norwegian and Icelandic cod.
The traditional ways of preparing the fish reflect the traditional
austerity of Norwegian life.

Typical of Denmark's cooking are their ways of preparing
eel. Some eel recipes are plain, and others are elaborate, combining eel with sauces or other foods. Americans have always
looked askance at eels. Yet I think at least smoked or curried eel
should be tried once; who knows, one may even get to like it! I
did, in Copenhagen.

As is the case in America, salmon is the noblest of all fish
throughout Scandinavia. Especially in Norway and in Iceland,
possession of a salmon stream means both personal joy and
money, the money coming from renting out the salmon waters
to Englishmen, Americans, and other affluent fishing enthusiasts.
Catching a large salmon seems to be an emotional experience as
well. An otherwise unemotional Norwegian friend told me that
she was completely overwhelmed when she held the first enormous salmon she had ever caught. As for me, I consider all fishing a bore, though I love eating fresh fish with a passion.

Scandinavian Basic Fish Stock for Poaching or Boiling Fish

ABOUT 2 QUARTS

Though many Scandinavians boil fish in plain salted water, far superior results are achieved with the use of this fish stock. When you're buying fish fillets, ask your market to give you the heads and bones of the fish for the stock.

2 quarts water
½ cup vinegar
1 stalk celery
3 large sprigs parsley or
  5 sprigs dill

Bones and heads of
  any white fish
12 peppercorns
1 small onion,
  quartered
1 teaspoon salt

Combine all ingredients and simmer, uncovered, 15 minutes. Strain liquid several times so that it will be clear. Cool stock before using it.

Norwegian and Icelandic Cod

Torsk

The best cod for boiling and baking is the big Lofoten cod. The smaller cod caught around the coast of Norway is preferred for pickling and smoking. It is considered essential to have absolutely fresh fish, preferably just caught.

Boiled cod is served with boiled potatoes, melted parsley

butter, or a mustard sauce. In Norway, *red* wine is served with cod, preferably a claret.

A memorable dinner given by Mr. L. Hegdahl of Trondheim consisted of boiled cod with potatoes and melted butter and an excellent Médoc. It was followed by cloudberries with whipped cream. The dinner was unforgettably good because of the unparalleled quality of the ingredients, and the care with which the fish was cooked. Each slice was boiled individually, and second helpings came on fresh, hot plates.

The following directions may seem to make quite a production of boiling a piece of fish. However, the excellence of a cook is shown when it comes to preparing simple food simply, without any sauces or furbelows to mask a less perfect basic preparation.

To prepare cod: Clean fish. Rinse inside thoroughly to remove any trace of the blood. For sliced fish, cut off head and reserve; also reserve roes and liver. Place fish, either whole or in slices, in a large bowl. Cover with ice cubes. Set under running water for 30 minutes to firm flesh. Drain and dry thoroughly with kitchen towel or kitchen paper before cooking.

To boil a whole cod: Place whole fish in cold water barely to cover. To each quart of water add 2 tablespoons salt. Bring to a quick boil. Simmer about 6 to 8 minutes to the pound, depending on size of fish. Do not overcook. The water must not boil—it must barely simmer. Lift out fish carefully and drain. Place on platter within folded napkin to keep hot; the cloth will also absorb excess moisture.

NOTE: To make handling of fish easier, wrap in a long piece of cheesecloth. Leave long ends at either side of cloth, to serve as handles. Keep the handles outside of the pot while the fish is cooking. Grasp them to lift out the fish.

To boil sliced cod: With sharp knife cut prepared fish into 1-inch slices. Set under ice and running water; drain and dry before cooking. In a large kettle boil water; add 2 tablespoons salt for each quart. (The water should be salty like sea water.)

Lower fish slices, including head, into boiling water. Let the water come to the boil once more. Simmer for 1 to 3 minutes, or until bone can be removed. Do not overcook. Remove fish carefully; drain. Place on folded napkin and remove skin. Garnish with sliced boiled roe.

To cook cod roe: Boil in salted water about 15 minutes.

To cook cod liver: Cut in small pieces and cook in as little water as possible for 15 to 20 minutes. Serve liver pieces in water; add 1 tablespoon of vinegar and some freshly ground pepper. (Eating the cod liver, which does not taste like the cod liver oil of our childhood, has kept Norwegians happy and healthy.)

FINAL NOTE: The top of the cod head, the jaw muscles, and the thick part of the neck are considered especially good.

Norwegian Pressed Cod

Persetorsk

A favorite Norwegian cod dish.

Cut off head of fish and cut fish down the back. Leave belly whole. Clean fish, wash thoroughly, and dry. Rub with coarse salt—about 1½ teaspoons for each pound of fish. Cover with salt the bottom of a bowl long enough to accommodate fish. Place fish on it. Sprinkle top of fish with more salt. Place a board or platter on fish to weigh it down. Keep in cold place for 2 to 3 days. Take up fish, drain, and wash. Place fish between two boards and put a stone or some heavy weight on top to flatten. Let stand another day. To cook, wash again and dry. Cut into 2-inch pieces. Cook in boiling unsalted water 2 to 3 minutes. Serve with cooked carrots, melted butter, and chopped hard-cooked egg.

Prince Fish

Prinsefisk

4 SERVINGS

---

1 ½ to 2 pounds cod fillets
  (if frozen, thaw first)
Milk
16 stalks asparagus,
  cooked, or canned or
  frozen asparagus,
  cooked according to
  package directions

2 cups hot medium-
  thick white sauce,
  made with half
  milk, half heavy
  cream
3 egg yolks

Place fish in buttered baking dish. Cover with milk. Bring to a
boil; simmer until fish is cooked and flaky, about 5 to 7 minutes
or less. Drain off milk. Arrange asparagus in lattice pattern over
fish. Beat egg yolks into hot white sauce. Pour sauce over fish
and asparagus. Place in broiler 2 to 3 minutes or until top is
browned and bubbly.

Fried Plaice or Flounder

3 TO 4 SERVINGS

Plaice is a flat fish. You also may use another flat fish such as
flounder.

6 small plaice or flounder,
  filleted, skinned,
  cleaned, and cut into
  serving pieces
Salt
Pepper

1 egg, well beaten
1 cup flour or fine dry
  bread crumbs
⅓ cup butter
Parsley or dill sprigs

Sprinkle fish with salt and pepper. Dip fillets into egg and roll in flour or bread crumbs. Heat butter in skillet. Fry fish until golden brown. Decorate platter with parsley or dill sprigs. Serve with browned butter and lemon wedges and boiled potatoes.

Plaice Surprise

Rødspaette Surprise

4 TO 6 SERVINGS

This is a spectacular dish Danish cooks turn out easily. In Denmark the fish is fried, but for greater ease of preparation I recommend the baking method. The results are about the same.

Since it is almost impossible to obtain plaice in America, I've made this dish with flounder, another flat fish.

1½-pound whole plaice or flounder
2 potatoes, peeled and sliced into finger lengths
Salt
½ cup flour
1 egg, well beaten
1 cup fine dry bread crumbs
½ cup salad oil or lard (for skillet method) or ½ cup butter (for baking method)

1 cup creamed chopped spinach
One 3-ounce jar tiny imported Danish shrimp or ½ cup tiny cooked and shelled fresh shrimp
Twelve 2-inch asparagus tips, cooked (canned, frozen, or fresh)

Skillet method: Skin fish and remove head. Slash fish on one side down the length of the backbone. Strip the fillets partially from the bone. Turn fillets out like lapels. Place raw potatoes into the pocket to hold the fillets in position. Sprinkle fish with salt. Let stand 10 minutes. Rinse fish, remove potatoes, and wipe fish dry. Coat entire fish with flour—including the turned-out fillets and the pocket. Dip fish into beaten egg, coating all the surfaces. Dip into bread crumbs and coat fish thoroughly. Heat salad oil or lard in a large skillet. Fry fish pocket side down until brown, making sure fillets are turned out. Fill pocket in the fish with a strip of creamed spinach, shrimp, and asparagus tips, arranged in a neat, decorative pattern.

Baking method: Prepare fish as above. Melt butter. Brush generously over a flat heatproof serving platter. Place fish on platter. Drizzle remaining melted butter over the whole fish, coating the entire surface. Hold lapels in place with toothpicks. Bake in 375° oven about 25 minutes or until golden brown and tender. Decorate with spinach, shrimp, and asparagus as described above.

NOTE: I know that it is difficult to imagine this dish without a picture. What it amounts to is a fish cut open and stuffed with spinach, shrimp, and asparagus, with two flaps at either side. Very colorful and Danish.

Scandinavian Poached Salmon

Scandinavian salmon is superlative. It is cooked and treated with the greatest reverence. Salmon can be cooked in boiled water, but for best results use a good court bouillon for poaching.

Fresh salmon, from 1-pound piece to whole fish

Court bouillon (recipe below)
Parsley or dill sprigs

In order to keep fish intact, wrap in cheesecloth, leaving long ends at either side that will serve as handles. Pour sufficient court bouillon to cover salmon in deep, long kettle or fish boiler. Place rack in kettle. Bring court bouillon to a boil, reduce heat so that liquid barely simmers. Lower fish on rack. Simmer, covered, about 7 to 8 minutes to the pound. If the fish is very large, allow an extra 5 to 10 minutes. Test for doneness by inserting thin skewer into center of fish. When fish is done, remove carefully from kettle. Unwrap; the skin should come off with the cheesecloth. Trim fish, or, if it is to be served whole, leave head and tail on. Transfer to hot platter; garnish with parsley or dill sprigs. Serve salmon with any standard béchamel or hollandaise, or with mustard or horseradish sauce, and with butter-steamed new potatoes.

COURT BOUILLON FOR SALMON
(or other fish)

Combine

3 quarts water

1 quart dry white wine

½ cup white vinegar

3 medium-size onions, cut
   in quarters

2 carrots, diced

½ stalk celery

1 bay leaf

5 sprigs fresh dill (or
1 ½ tablespoons
dill seeds) or
parsley, preferably
dill

Bring to a boil and simmer, covered, for 1 hour. Strain before using to poach fish.

Norwegian Fried Salmon or Trout

Ristet Laks eller Ørret

4 SERVINGS

This is much better than the usual fried salmon or trout.

2 pounds salmon steaks,
   or trout, prepared
   for cooking
1 ½ teaspoons salt
¼ teaspoon pepper
2 tablespoons olive oil

2 tablespoons white
   vinegar
1 tablespoon fish stock
   or dry white wine
1 egg, slightly beaten
Dry bread crumbs
Butter

Place fish in shallow baking dish forming one layer. Combine salt, pepper, olive oil, vinegar, and fish stock or wine. Sprinkle over fish. Let stand 2 hours. Baste occasionally with marinade. Drain fish and dry thoroughly. Coat with beaten egg and bread crumbs. Melt butter in skillet to the depth of ¼ inch. Place fish in skillet, side by side. Do not crowd. Fry over low heat until browned at the bottom. Carefully turn over with broad spatula. Add more butter, if necessary; the pan should not be dry. Continue cooking until browned. Serve on hot dish, garnished with lemon. Serve melted parsley butter separately. Boiled potatoes are the best and usual accompaniment.

Swedish Marinated Salmon

Gravad Lax

ABOUT 12 TO 15 SERVINGS

I wish to sing the praises of this wonderful dish. *Gravad lax* is used like smoked salmon (it looks like it, too), but it is infinitely more delicate in flavor. In fact, it is salmon at its best. This dish is not cooked, which may surprise my readers. But I know that anybody who has once tried *gravad lax*, which is exceedingly easy to make, will want to make it again and again for the most elegant parties.

Important: You must have plenty of fresh dill for *gravad lax*. Nothing else will do. Also, you must use fresh salmon that has not been frozen, or the dish will be a failure. The action of the seasonings on the fresh fish is what gives it its fine texture and flavor.

7 to 8 pounds fresh salmon in one piece, with bones in	1 teaspoon whole allspice, crushed
⅔ cup salt	6 tablespoons Cognac
½ cup sugar	2 large bunches of fresh dill
1 tablespoon whole white pepper, crushed	

Buy middle cut from salmon. Clean fish, leaving skin on. Carefully remove bone so that two big fillets remain. Rinse in iced water and carefully dry with kitchen towel, taking care that fish does not break. Mix together salt, sugar, pepper, and allspice. Rub seasonings carefully into all sides of the fish. Sprinkle with Cognac. Wash dill and place one third of it in bottom of deep bowl. Use an enamel, china, stone, or stainless-steel bowl, but not an aluminum one. Place one piece of salmon, skin side down, on the dill. Place another third of the dill on the salmon and top with second piece of salmon, skin side up. Cover with remaining dill. Set heavy plate or board on salmon. Refrigerate no less than 24 hours, and preferably, 36 hours. Drain fish, scrape off dill and spices, and slice thinly on the slant, away from the skin. Serve with lemon wedges, mustard sauce and plenty of freshly ground black pepper.

NOTE: *Gravad lax* will keep about 8 days in the refrigerator, wrapped in aluminum foil.

For an extra Scandinavian touch, cut skin of *gravad lax* into half-inch strips. Fry in hot butter until crisp and serve with salmon.

If *gravad lax* is not part of the smorgasbord but a course in itself, it is served with steamed potatoes with butter sauce and cucumber salad, and is accompanied as well by a mustard sauce.

Swedish Salmon Aspic

From Paul Debry who runs Corn Products, Inc., in Sweden and hobnobs with the best cooks, such as one of the chefs for the king of Sweden.

2 quarts water
1 ½ tablespoons white
    vinegar
1 ½ teaspoons salt
5 sprigs dill or
    1 tablespoon dill seed
8 peppercorns
8 whole allspice
2 bay leaves
1 pound fresh or frozen
    salmon
¾ pound shrimp,
    shelled and deveined
2 unbeaten egg whites

4 envelopes unflavored
    gelatin (about 4
    tablespoons)
½ cup cold water
2 tablespoons lemon
    juice
½ teaspoon salt
¼ teaspoon pepper
2 hard-cooked eggs,
    cut in quarters
¼ cup mayonnaise
Cucumber slices
Watercress
Dill sprigs
Dill mayonnaise

Combine water, vinegar, salt, dill, peppercorns, allspice, and bay leaves in large kettle. Bring to a boil and boil 5 minutes. Wrap salmon in cheesecloth and place in boiling water. Reduce heat and simmer 5 minutes. Add shrimp; simmer until shrimp are pink and fish flakes, about 5 minutes. Remove fish and shrimp; reserve. Strain stock into saucepan and add egg whites. Bring to a boil slowly, stirring constantly. Remove from heat; cover and let stand 15 minutes. Strain through double thickness of cheesecloth and measure 1½ quarts. Sprinkle gelatin on cold water; soften for 5 minutes. Add to hot stock and stir until gelatin is completely dissolved. Add lemon juice, salt, and pepper. Pour enough mixture into a 9- by 9- by 1¾-inch pan to form a ⅛-inch layer. Chill until set. Arrange shrimp and hard-cooked eggs, cut side down, in a decorative pattern on the chilled gelatin. Blend mayonnaise with 1½ cups of the remaining gelatin. Pour over shrimp and egg; chill until set. Flake salmon into bite-size pieces. Arrange on mayonnaise-gelatin layer. Pour on remaining gelatin. Chill until set. Unmold on serving platter. Garnish with cucumber slices and watercress and decorate with dill. Serve with additional mayonnaise, diluted with lemon juice to taste, and mixed with dill.

Norwegian Trout

Ørret

Excellent freshwater or sea trout abounds in Norway, land of innumerable streams and endless coastal waters. The Norwegian housewife, who likes to buy her trout live (as well as other fish), never washes it since washing softens the flesh, a suggestion worth adapting in America. To clean trout, remove the head and draw out the entrails. With a long, thin knife, loosen the tissue over the backbone and sides of the belly. Clean the fish with paper towels, then dry well with paper towels. Stuff a clean piece of paper towel into the fish until it is ready to be cooked. Boil, or panfry in butter, and serve with boiled potatoes, melted parsley butter, and cucumber salad.

Norwegian Corned Trout

Rakørret

This is a Norwegian national dish, beloved by the natives, though the foreigners take to it with caution. Personally, I learned to like it, like Scotch whisky. I have not made this dish, but since it belongs in a book with typical dishes, I take this recipe from Mrs. Sverdrup's cookbook *Norwegian Delight*. She tells me that it is a cinch.

A 1- to 2-pound fish is a good size for corning. Clean; sprinkle head and body cavity with salt. Arrange fish in a wide-mouthed stone crock or small wooden barrel, belly side up. Sprinkle salt and 1 teaspoon sugar over each layer of fish. Weigh layers down with a plate with a weight on it to form juice. The juice should cover the fish completely. Keep in a cool place 3 months. Drain, and serve very cold with thin rye bread and butter. Beer and *snaps* is a must with this lordly repast, says Mrs. Sverdrup.

NOTE: The canny Norwegians corn their trout at the end of August when the fish are fat.

Scandinavian Boiled Lobster

Kokt Hummer

---

1 live lobster
4 quarts water
5 tablespoons salt

1 bunch of dill, tied
together

Lobster is a great favorite, especially in Sweden. To cook, plunge the lobster into boiling water, seasoned with salt and dill. Allow the water to return to a boil. Reduce the heat at once and simmer the lobster 5 minutes for the first pound and about 3 minutes for each additional pound. Drain. Serve lobster with mayonnaise or any cold sauce, including Danish sharp sauce (see page 154).

Swedish Lobster Soufflé

Hummersuffle

3 SERVINGS

---

3 tablespoons butter
3 tablespoons flour
1 cup light cream, heated
6 eggs, separated
½ teaspoon salt
¼ teaspoon white
pepper

1 cup chopped lobster
meat
1 tablespoon chopped
dill
Butter
Fine dry bread
crumbs (optional)

Set oven at 350°.

Melt butter and blend in flour. Add cream gradually, stirring constantly, and cook until mixture is smooth and thick. Cool sauce. Beat in egg yolks, one at a time. Season with salt and pepper. Fold lobster and dill into mixture. Beat egg whites until stiff but not dry and fold into lobster mixture. Butter a 2-quart soufflé dish and coat it with fine dry bread crumbs. (The bread crumbs are optional, but they are used in Sweden.) Pour soufflé mixture into dish and bake about 30 to 40 minutes, or until puffed and golden. Serve immediately, with steamed potatoes and melted butter or hollandaise.

NOTE: Though the quantities of the lobster soufflé can be doubled, it is far better to make 2 smaller soufflés rather than 1 large one. Smaller soufflés bake better.

Scandinavian Crabmeat Aspic

ABOUT 12 SERVINGS

Handsome for the smorgasbord table.

1 large-size package (6 ounces) lemon-flavored gelatin
4 chicken bouillon cubes
1 teaspoon salt
2 cups boiling water
3 tablespoons lemon juice
2 tablespoons Cognac or ⅓ cup lemon juice
¼ teaspoon white pepper

2 cups sour cream
2 teaspoons grated onion
2 cups flaked fresh or canned crabmeat
1 cup chopped celery
3 tablespoons chopped dill or parsley
Lettuce
Tomato slices

Dissolve gelatin, bouillon cubes, and salt in boiling water. Add lemon juice and Cognac (or additional ⅓ cup lemon juice), pepper, sour cream, and grated onion. Blend thoroughly. Chill until slightly thickened. Then fold in crabmeat, celery, and dill. Pour into a rinsed 2-quart mold or individual molds. Chill until firm. Unmold on a bed of crisp lettuce and garnish with tomato slices. Serve with cucumber mayonnaise (see page 28).

Swedish and Finnish Crayfish

5 TO 6 SERVINGS

The beginning of the crayfish season in August is a national event in Sweden, celebrated with special parties and much akvavit and beer. It is an annual ritual.

Crayfish are not shrimp; they resemble lobsters, but are much smaller.

Crayfish are boiled in a simple court bouillon. As they are eaten, the heads should be laid side by side in a circle along the outer edges of the plate. The outermost tip of the bill, cut with a tiny knife, is considered a special delicacy.

Like lobster, crayfish should be alive before boiling.

40 to 50 crayfish	*1 bunch of dill, tied*
4 quarts water	*together*
5 tablespoons salt	*Dill sprigs*

Wash crayfish thoroughly in fresh water. Pull off the tiny wing in the center of the tail. Combine water, salt, and dill in a large pot. Bring to a boil and boil 5 minutes. Place 10 crayfish into boiling water. Let boil and remove crayfish when red. Remove crayfish to tray. Bring water again to a rapid boil and add next 10 shellfish. Repeat process with remaining crayfish. Cool crayfish in stock and leave standing for 1 to 2 hours. Drain, arrange on platter, and decorate with dill sprigs.

> NOTE: Shrimp can be cooked in this manner, with excellent results. Cook 3 to 5 minutes depending on size. Tiny shrimp should be plunged in boiling court bouillon, withdrawn from heat and cooled in bouillon. This will cook them through, but preserve their texture.

Danish Fried Eels with Creamed Potatoes

Stegt Aal med Stuvede Kartofler

4 TO 6 SERVINGS

A Danish classic. Eels, when properly cooked as they are in Denmark, are delicious, and Americans would do well to overcome their prejudice against them.

3 large eels	2 cups milk
Salt	1 teaspoon grated
1 ¾ cups flour	lemon rind
2 eggs, beaten	½ teaspoon white
1 ½ cups fine dry	pepper
bread crumbs	2 tablespoons minced
⅓ cup plus ¼ cup butter	parsley
6 medium-size potatoes,	
peeled and cubed	

Skin eels by cutting the skin around the head and peeling it back very slowly. You may need a pair of pliers to get started. Remove intestines from skinned eels and cut off the head. Cut eels into 3-inch pieces. Wash fish thoroughly and dry. Sprinkle with salt and let stand for 1 hour. Rinse with cold water and dry thoroughly. Roll eels in 1½ cups flour, then in beaten egg, and last in bread crumbs. Melt ⅓ cup butter in a skillet. Fry eels in it about 20 minutes, or until golden brown and tender. Turn fish occasionally. Cook potatoes in boiling salt water until tender. Drain; keep hot. Melt ¼ cup butter and stir in ¼ cup flour. Gradually add milk, stirring constantly. Cook over low heat until sauce is thickened and smooth. Stir in 1 teaspoon salt, lemon rind, and pepper. Pour sauce over potatoes. Surround potatoes with fried eel pieces. Sprinkle with parsley.

NOTE: The Danes say that you must eat sufficient eel to make a ring around the plate with the bones.

Werner Christiansen's Singapore Eel

4 TO 6 SERVINGS

Mr. Christiansen had a famous restaurant, the Coq d'Or in Copenhagen.

3 pounds fresh eels, cleaned and skinned	1 ½ cups diced, skinned fresh tomatoes
¼ cup butter	1 ½ teaspoons salt
2 tablespoons curry powder, or more	¼ teaspoon freshly ground black
¼ cup minced onion	pepper
1 cup diced carrots	½ cup water or fish
1 cup diced celery	stock, or more
1 cup diced mushrooms	1 cup dry white wine

Cut eels into 1½-inch pieces. Heat butter in deep kettle and stir in curry powder. Cook over medium heat 3 minutes, stirring constantly. Add onion, carrots, celery, mushrooms, tomatoes, and stir thoroughly. Add eel, salt and pepper, water or fish stock, and white wine. Simmer, covered, over low heat about 18 to 20 minutes, stirring occasionally. Check for moisture; if too thick, add a little more water or wine. If too thin, thicken with a little flour. Serve with fluffy dry rice.

NOTE: This dish can also be made with shrimp. In this case, the sauce should simmer for about 15 minutes before adding the raw shrimp (which have been shelled and deveined) and cooked 7 to 10 minutes longer, depending on the size of the shrimp.

Scandinavian Pickled Herring

A universal favorite, both on the cold table and as a meal, when it is served with boiled potatoes and a sauce, such as mustard or horseradish. Dark bread and sweet butter are natural companions for this herring.

3 to 4 salted herring (from
    fish and specialty
    markets; they come
    packed in salt brine)
Milk
Water
⅔ cup wine vinegar

⅓ cup sugar
2 teaspoons ground
    allspice (optional)
2 medium-size onions,
    sliced
¼ cup sherry
    (optional)

Wash herring thoroughly in running cold water. Place in deep bowl and cover with equal parts of milk and water. Let stand overnight. Drain herring and dry. Cut off heads and trim away darkened edge of neck. Fillet herring, but do not remove skin. Trim bottom and side of each fillet to remove fins; cut away top fin. Cut fillets crosswise into ½-inch strips and set aside small tail ends. Combine wine vinegar, 1 cup water, sugar, and allspice and bring to a boil. Cool. In wide-mouthed quart-size jar or bowl place a layer of the tail pieces. Cover with onions. Repeat process, making alternate layers of herring and onions. Pour marinade over fish. Cover tightly. Let stand 2 to 3 days before using. At serving time drain fish and sprinkle sherry over it.

NOTE: This is but one version of dozens of pickled herrings. Essentially there is not much difference between recipes and the results are about the same.

Swedish Fried Herring or Smelt Fillets

Stekt Strömming

4 SERVINGS

Excellent also when made with filleted mackerel.

2 pounds herring or
  smelt fillets
1 teaspoon salt
¼ teaspoon white pepper
½ cup butter

1 cup chopped parsley
  or ½ cup chopped
  dill
2 eggs, beaten
2 cups fine dry
  bread crumbs

Wash fish fillets in iced water. Dry on paper towels. Sprinkle with salt and pepper. Blend together ¼ cup of the butter with the parsley or dill. Spread on fish fillets and put together like a sandwich. Dip fish sandwiches in beaten eggs and roll in bread crumbs. Shake free of excess crumbs. Chill for 15 to 30 minutes. (This is not strictly necessary, but fish fries more easily.) Melt remaining butter and fry fish sandwiches in it until golden on all sides. Serve with mashed potatoes and a salad.

Variation
PICKLED FRIED HERRING OR SMELTS

Inlagd Stekt Strömming

¾ cup white vinegar
¼ cup water
2 tablespoons sugar
5 peppercorns
1 medium-size onion,
   sliced

5 large dill sprigs
Fried herring or
   smelts (see above)
   made with dill,
   cold

Combine vinegar, water, sugar, peppercorns, onion, and dill. Bring to a boil; simmer, covered, 5 to 10 minutes. Strain and chill. Pour over fried fish and chill in refrigerator for 3 hours or overnight. Drain before serving. Very good for a smorgasbord.

Scandinavian Baked Perch or Pike with Parsley and Dill

4 SERVINGS

---

8 medium-size perch or
   pike, dressed
1 teaspoon salt
½ teaspoon pepper
Butter
½ cup minced parsley

½ cup minced dill or
   1 tablespoon dill
   seed
¼ cup boiling water
Parsley and dill sprigs
Cucumber slices
Lemon slices

Set oven at 350°.

Sprinkle fish with salt and pepper. Butter a shallow baking dish. Place half of the minced parsley and dill on bottom of baking dish. Top with fish laid in a row. Cover fish with remaining parsley and dill. Pour water around fish. Bake 20 minutes or more, depending on size of fish, or until fish flakes. Transfer fish to hot serving platter and garnish with sprigs of parsley and dill, cucumber and lemon slices. Serve with boiled potatoes and a sauce of melted butter.

Norwegian Fish Pudding

Fiskepudding or Fiskefarse

Fish pudding is served in Norway at least once a week. Cold, it is either sliced and warmed in butter, or eaten as a sandwich topping. This pudding, which is one of the most typical of Norwegian dishes, should be snow white, light but firm, with a somewhat spongy consistency. It is always made with fresh fish, and it is usually served with a melted butter sauce, or a shrimp, lobster, or tomato sauce. The pudding is very delicate and excellent.

Making fish pudding in the traditional way is a very laborious job. It is much easier done in the electric blender or food processor. When steaming the fish pudding, the water in which the mold sits should be barely simmering. It must not boil, or the pudding will have holes.

Butter
Bread crumbs
2 pounds white fish,
  preferably cod or
  haddock (in Norway
  cod is usually used),
  without skin or bones

1 tablespoon salt
2 tablespoons
  cornstarch
1 cup light cream or
  milk
1 cup heavy cream

Butter a 1½-quart mold or casserole. Dust with bread crumbs. Check fish to be sure that no bones remain. Sprinkle fish with salt; cut into pieces. Push fish once through the finest blade of a meat grinder. Slowly stir in cornstarch, and grind four times more. Mix together light cream and heavy cream. Stir in cream very slowly, beating well all the time. (The slow addition of the cream and its proper incorporation is the secret of a good fish pudding.) The mixture should be fluffy. Pour into buttered mold and smooth top.

Cover mold with its own cover, or butter some aluminum foil or nonwaxed paper, cover mold, and tie. Set mold in pan of simmering water, which should come three quarters of the way to the top of the mold. The water must not boil. Steam about 1 hour or until a silver knife blade inserted into fish pudding comes out clean. Unmold on hot plate; drain. Serve with lobster or shrimp sauce or melted butter.

The pudding can also be set in a shallow pan with water and baked in a moderate oven (350°) for about 50 minutes or until it tests done.

NOTE: The prepared fish mixture can also be shaped with 2 spoons into small balls and poached for a few minutes in simmering water. Or it may be shaped into flat cakes and fried in butter.

Do not attempt to serve fish pudding to company if you've never made it before. It is a delicate dish and requires a little practice. Also, some recipes call for butter and eggs, not indigenous to traditional *fiskepudding*. In this case it loses its snow-white beauty and becomes a soufflé.

Blender or food processor method: Cut prepared fish into small pieces. Place a few pieces at a time into blender or processor container and purée at high speed. Do not attempt to purée more than a few pieces at a time. Beat cornstarch into fish. Divide fish and cream into 4 portions each. Blend at high speed 1 portion fish and 1 portion cream at a time. Transfer blended portion to bowl and repeat until all fish and cream are used. Beat mixture vigorously with slotted spoon for ½ minute. Cook as above.

Fish Gratin

Fiskegratin

Popular throughout Scandinavia, made with either fresh or left-over fish. This particular version comes from Captain F. Krist-jansen, an inspector of the Bergen Line, with whom I sailed around northern Norway. This gentleman is a *bon vivant*, with winning ways.

*2 pounds fish fillets (cod,
haddock, plaice,
flounder, pike, etc.)
1 ¾ teaspoons salt
¾ teaspoon white pepper
¼ cup lemon juice
11 tablespoons butter
6 tablespoons flour
3 cups light cream,
heated*

*3 egg yolks
1 cup cooked, shelled
and deveined
shrimp, coarsely
chopped
1 cup cooked lobster,
chopped
¼ cup grated
Parmesan cheese*

Set oven at 350°.

Place fillets in buttered 2-quart baking dish. Sprinkle with 1 teaspoon salt, ½ teaspoon pepper and lemon juice. Dot with 2 tablespoons butter. Cover dish with aluminum foil or lid and bake about 20 minutes, or until fish flakes. While fish is baking, make sauce. Heat 6 tablespoons butter and stir in flour. Cook until smooth, but do not let brown. Gradually stir in hot cream, and cook over low heat until sauce is thick and smooth, stirring constantly. Remove from heat and beat in egg yolks, one at a time, and remaining 3 tablespoons butter. Season with ¾ teaspoon salt and ¼ teaspoon pepper. Sauce must be very smooth and hot. Remove foil or cover from fish and drain off excess liquid. Top fish with shrimp and lobster. Pour hot sauce over fish and sprinkle with Parmesan cheese. Set dish on broiler rack 4 to 5 inches away from source of heat. Broil about 2 to 3 minutes until golden brown.

Boiled Swedish Lutfisk

A must for a Scandinavian, especially for a Swedish Christmas. Lutfisk is cod treated with lime, and in the old days this treatment took place at home. Now even the Swedish housewife buys her lutfisk prepared for cooking. In America, Scandinavian delicatessens will have lutfisk at Christmas time.

3 pounds prepared lutfisk, cut in serving pieces	*Freshly ground black pepper*
Salt	*Mustard*
Boiling water, about ½ cup	*Ground allspice*

Lutfisk is delicate to handle and it is best to place the pieces in a piece of cheescloth, tying the ends.

Boil salt and water in large deep frying pan. Add lutfisk, either wrapped in a cheesecloth or in pieces, skin side down. Cover pan and bring to a simmering, not boiling point. Simmer about 10 to 15 minutes or until fish flakes easily. Lift out fish carefully and drain well. Place on hot platter and remove skin and fins. Serve with freshly ground black pepper, a pinch of mustard and a pinch of allspice; also serve boiled potatoes and cream sauce. (These are the classic Swedish Christmas foods to go with lutfisk.)

Baked Lutfisk

Set oven at 300°.

Place prepared lutfisk, skin side down, in a large shallow baking dish. Sprinkle with about 2 tablespoons water. Bake about 30 minutes. Serve as above.

BIRDS AND MEATS

*T*he best Scandinavian meat and fowl dishes are to my mind the Danish and Swedish ones, because of the natural resources and the historical traditions of the two countries. Both Denmark and Sweden have much better animal resources than Norway, Finland, and Iceland, and both Denmark and Sweden also always had a higher standard of living, thanks to their natural resources. Added to this is the fact that both Denmark and Sweden were ruled by royalty, whose fancier cuisines trickled down to the classes below them, and these lower classes were always eager to imitate their so-called betters in every way they could. Denmark has always been the freest—in living habits, at least—of all Scandinavian countries, and there, to this day, people go to eat and drink well. Sweden used to be one of Europe's most powerful states, whose politics affected the European continent. Can we then be surprised that Sweden was looked up to if not in her politics, at least in her ways of living?

Birds and meat have always been rich eating, but rich eating conditioned by the availability of the meats. Hence the predominance of pork in simple or festive forms, since pigs are animals that do not require much land to thrive. Pigs can be kept in pens, too, a definite advantage when the winters are long and cold. Pigs can be easily handled without professional help, and their meat is easy to preserve by whoever raised them. Finally, pigs are easy to feed, since they will eat swill. . . . In other words, pork was the natural meat of the small homesteader, and not only in Scandinavia, but in the early United States and in as different a country as China.

Sweden has more pasture lands on which to graze cattle, and thus Sweden's beef dishes are, to my mind, the ones that not only appeal most to our tastes but are the best. Modern Swedish chefs manage imaginatively to embroider the traditional meat recipes of their country with superb results.

Finland's traditional meat cookery is a combination of pork and more costly meats; her fancier traditional dishes are, as usual, inspired by Sweden and Russia's elegant court cookery. In Iceland, as in much of Scandinavia, especially in Norway, the festive meat is lamb; young lambs do not require pasturage before adulthood, and their meat is extremely tasty.

As for chicken, before assembly-line produced chickens made it a cheap meat, it was festive fare, served with a rich sauce throughout Scandinavia.

Scandinavian Roast Chicken

4 SERVINGS

Scandinavians roast their chickens not in the oven, but in a heavy pan on top of the stove. Parsley is a favorite stuffing, and cream sauce is the standard chicken sauce.

One 3- to 4-pound whole
   roasting chicken
2 teaspoons salt
½ teaspoon white pepper
6 tablespoons butter

1 to 1½ cups chopped
   parsley
1 cup chicken
   bouillon, or more,
   boiling
Sauce (recipe below)

Rub chicken inside and out with salt and pepper. Mix half of the butter with the parsley. Stuff chicken with mixture; truss. Heat remaining butter in heavy casserole or Dutch oven. Brown chicken in it on all sides. Cover with boiling bouillon. Simmer, covered tightly, for 40 to 50 minutes or until chicken is tender. Check occasionally for dryness; if necessary, add a little more boiling bouillon. Transfer chicken to hot serving platter and keep hot while making sauce.

Sauce

3 tablespoons pan
  drippings
3 tablespoons flour
1 cup broth from pan (if
  there is not sufficient
  broth, add boiling
  bouillon to make 1 cup)

⅔ cup heavy cream
Salt and pepper to
  taste
Pinch of ground
  cardamom
  (optional)

Heat pan drippings and stir in flour. Cook until golden, stirring constantly. Gradually stir in boiling broth and cook until thickened and smooth, stirring all the time. Reduce heat to lowest possible level and add cream. Season to taste. Simmer, covered, for 5 minutes, stirring occasionally. Strain and reheat.

NOTE: For a richer sauce add 3 tablespoons softened butter to heated strained sauce, beating vigorously until butter is absorbed.

To serve, decorate chicken platter with leaves of Boston lettuce, slices of tomato, and parsley sprigs. Serve sauce separately. Browned potatoes and a tossed green salad would complement the roast chicken.

Norwegian Chicken with Sour Cream

Stekt Kylling med Sur Fløte

3 TO 4 SERVINGS

This comes from Leif Borthen, a hospitable Oslo journalist who has done much to promote the cause of sophisticated cooking, both in word and deed.

One 3-pound frying
    chicken (about), cut
    in serving pieces
1 teaspoon salt
½ teaspoon white pepper
¼ cup butter
¼ cup Cognac
2 cups milk

¼ cup sherry
¼ cup chopped
    parsley
½ cup sour cream
Mushroom caps
    sautéed in butter
Broiled tomato halves
Parsley sprigs

Skin chicken and rub with salt and pepper. Heat butter in large, heavy skillet. Brown chicken in it on all sides. Flame by pouring Cognac over chicken and lighting the heated spirit. When the flame has died down, cover with milk. Simmer, covered, over lowest possible heat about 35 to 45 minutes or until chicken is tender. Baste occasionally with the milk, which will clot. Add sherry and parsley and cook 3 minutes longer. Transfer chicken pieces to hot platter and keep hot. Stir sour cream into pan juices and pour sauce over chicken. Garnish with mushroom caps, broiled tomato halves, and sprigs of parsley.

Danish Chicken Breasts Soubise

4 TO 6 SERVINGS

6 whole chicken breasts,
skinned and boned (the
butcher will do this)
1 quart chicken bouillon,
boiling
6 tablespoons butter
3 large onions, sliced as
thinly as possible
4 tablespoons butter

¼ cup Cognac
1 tablespoon flour
½ teaspoon salt
¼ teaspoon white pepper
⅓ cup heavy cream
2 medium-size truffles,
peeled (optional)
Parsley sprigs

Place chicken breasts in heavy casserole or Dutch oven and cover with boiling chicken bouillon. Add the first 6 tablespoons of butter. Cover tightly and simmer 30 minutes or until done. Drain; keep hot and reserve stock. Meanwhile, cook onions in heavy saucepan with 2 tablespoons of the butter for 15 minutes. Cook over lowest possible heat, stirring frequently. Onions must not become brown but should remain white. After 10 minutes of cooking time, stir in Cognac. Sprinkle with flour, salt, and pepper, and cook 3 minutes longer. Add ¾ cup of reserved chicken stock and simmer, covered, over lowest possible heat for 1 hour and 15 minutes. The onions must be simmered for this length of time and they must be kept as white as possible. Rub onion mixture through fine sieve or purée in blender. Place in top of double boiler and add cream. Taste and correct seasonings. Add remaining butter and stir until completely melted. Coat hot chicken breasts with part of the sauce and decorate with truffle cutouts. To serve, place chicken breasts on heated platter. Surround with mounds of buttered baby peas and carrots, and small browned potatoes. Decorate with parsley sprigs. Serve remaining sauce separately.

Norwegian Ptarmigan or Snow Bird

Ryper

4 SERVINGS

A great delicacy from the Arctic, justly admired by all of Scandinavia. The birds are usually cooked in the same way in all the countries. This version comes from the Prinsen Hotel in Trondheim, a handsome hotel that has several excellent restaurants with mile-long menu cards offering an international cuisine done up with a lavish hand, as well as a fine cellar.

Ptarmigan can be bought occasionally in American specialty stores. The following recipe is equally successful with other birds, such as grouse, quail, and snipe.

Game birds must be well larded or covered with fat during cooking or they tend to become dry.

4 ptarmigan
4 large slices of bacon or
   salt pork
1 teaspoon salt
½ teaspoon white pepper
1 cup butter
1 cup boiling water

1 cup hot milk
1 to 1½ cups sour
   cream or sweet
   heavy cream
2 slices of Norwegian
   goat cheese or ½
   cup blue cheese

Clean birds, wash, and dry. Tie a slice of bacon around the breast of each bird and fasten with toothpick or skewer. Or else, lift skin of the breast and insert bacon under the skin. Tie legs to the body. Sprinkle with salt and pepper. Reserve 1 tablespoon of the butter. Heat remaining butter in deep skillet. Brown birds in it on all sides. Gradually add the boiling water. Simmer, covered, over low heat for 15 minutes and then add hot milk. Simmer for 1½ to 3 hours, depending on the age and size of the birds. Keep skillet covered except for a crack to allow steam to escape. When meat shrinks away from the bones and birds are nearly done, stir in sour cream. Birds should cook about 30 minutes in sour cream. Transfer cooked birds to hot serving dish and keep hot. Bring gravy to a boil and add cheese. Check for seasoning. If gravy is too thick, dilute with a little hot water; if too thin, add a little more sour cream. Stir remaining tablespoon of butter into gravy. Pour gravy over birds. Serve with green peas or other vegetables, boiled potatoes, and lingonberry or cranberry preserves.

NOTE: It is considered a sin to put even a speck of flour into a first class ptarmigan gravy.

Swedish Royal Pot Roast

Slottsstek

4 TO 6 SERVINGS

Excellent. The anchovies give it its subtle flavor, which is not at all fishy.

4 pounds beef, chuck
    or round
2 teaspoons salt
1 teaspoon ground allspice
½ teaspoon pepper
3 tablespoons butter
3 tablespoons brandy
    or whisky
⅓ cup hot bouillon
2 medium-size onions,
    sliced

3 minced anchovy
    fillets, or 1 teaspoon
    anchovy paste
2 bay leaves
2 tablespoons white
    vinegar
2 tablespoons molasses
    or dark syrup
Tomato slices
Cucumber slices
Parsley sprigs
Gravy (recipe below)

Rub meat with salt, allspice, and pepper. Heat butter and brown meat in it on all sides. Pour brandy over hot meat and flame. Add bouillon, onions, anchovies, bay leaves, vinegar, and molasses and blend. Simmer covered over very low heat about 2 hours, or until meat is tender. Remove meat to hot serving platter and keep hot. Make gravy. Slice meat and surround with little mounds of buttered peas, carrots, and cauliflower buds, and decorate with tomato and cucumber slices and parsley. Pour a little of the gravy over the meat and serve the rest of the gravy separately.

Gravy

Make gravy from pan drippings in usual manner. Flavor with ¼ teaspoon anchovy paste and fold in 1 cup heavy cream, whipped.

Finnish Sour Pot Roast

4 SERVINGS

A kind of sauerbraten, but flavored more interestingly with beer, horseradish, and juniper berries. In Finland, fresh horseradish and a juniper branch with berries are *de rigueur*.

One 4-pound beef round
2 quarts beer
2 cups cider vinegar
1 cup sugar
1 teaspoon salt
1 teaspoon whole
    peppercorns
½ teaspoon ground
    or 1 teaspoon whole
    allspice
One ½-inch piece ginger-
    root or ½ teaspoon
    ground ginger
One ½-inch piece fresh
    horseradish or 2
    teaspoons bottled
    horseradish
12 juniper berries,
    crushed

Trim beef of excess fat. Combine all other ingredients. Place meat in deep bowl. (Do not use an aluminum bowl.) Pour marinade over meat. Let stand in refrigerator for 5 days. Rinse, dry, and pot-roast in the usual manner.

Scandinavian Seaman's Beef

Sjömansbiff

3 TO 4 SERVINGS

This is the Swedish version, and a very good one, of a popular Scandinavian dish. This casserole lends itself to informal buffet entertaining when hearty food is needed. Though the preparation takes a little time, this can be done in the morning, or the night before the casserole is to be served. Also, the beef does not suffer if kept waiting.

2 pounds chuck or round, or other boneless beef
1 ½ teaspoons salt
1 tablespoon freshly ground pepper
6 bay leaves, crumbled
One 12-ounce can of beer or ale, or more

⅓ cup flour
⅔ to 1 cup butter
2 pounds raw potatoes, peeled and sliced
3 large raw carrots, sliced
3 large onions, sliced

Cut meat into thin 1-inch squares about ¼ inch thick. Sprinkle with salt and pepper. Place in deep container and sprinkle with crumbled bay leaves. Pour beer over meat. Let stand 4 hours or overnight.

Set oven at 350°.

Drain meat and dry. Reserve beer marinade. Coat meat

with flour. Heat one third of the butter and fry meat over high heat until golden on both sides. Reserve meat. Fry potatoes in the same skillet for 3 minutes and reserve. Add more butter and fry carrots for 3 minutes and reserve. Add remaining butter and fry onions until soft and golden. Arrange alternate layers of potatoes, meat, carrots, and onions in buttered 2½-quart casserole. The first and last layers should be potatoes. Pour reserved beer marinade over meat mixture. Cover with lid or aluminum foil and bake about 1½ hours or until meat and vegetables are tender. Check occasionally for moisture; if too dry, add a little more beer, about ⅓ cup at a time. Serve with a tossed green salad or with sliced tomatoes and cucumbers.

Swedish Beef Lindström

3 TO 4 SERVINGS

A piquant hamburger that is extremely good. The patties should be large and flat.

2 pounds ground steak
3 egg yolks
¾ cup mashed potatoes
2 teaspoons salt
½ teaspoon pepper
¼ cup heavy cream

¾ cup cooked beets
(or pickled beets),
finely chopped
⅓ cup finely
chopped onion
⅓ cup capers,
chopped
Butter

Blend together meat, egg yolks, mashed potatoes, salt, and pepper. Gradually beat in cream. Combine beets, onion, and capers and blend into mixture. Shape into large flat patties and fry quickly in butter on both sides.

NOTE: In Sweden, Beef Lindström is often served with a fried egg on top.

Danish Boneless Birds

Benløse Fugle

This dish, with variations, is found in all Scandinavian countries. The Danish bacon is sold canned throughout the country and is very tasty.

Danish bacon or salt pork,   *Salt*
   cut in strips a little   *Pepper*
   shorter than length   *Minced parsley*
   of meat   *Butter*
Round steak cut in   *Boiling bouillon*
   ½-inch-thick   *Flour, cream for*
   slices, 2 per person   *gravy*

If salt pork is used, soak in cold water if too salty. Dry before using. Pound meat thin with meat pounder or rolling pin. Season with salt and pepper. Use little salt, since bacon or pork are salty. Place a strip of bacon on each slice of beef, and top with a teaspoon of minced parsley. Roll up and fasten with toothpicks. Melt butter and fry birds on all sides until brown. Add boiling bouillon to cover. Simmer, covered, for 1 hour or until meat is tender. Transfer meat to heated platter and keep hot. Make cream gravy in the usual manner. Pour sauce over meat or serve separately. Serve with new potatoes sprinkled with parsley and cucumber salad.

Norwegian Breaded Breast of Veal

3 TO 4 SERVINGS

Inexpensive and very good family food.

*3 to 4 pounds breast
  of veal
Boiling water
1 tablespoon salt
2 egg whites, slightly
  beaten*

*1 cup fine dry
  bread crumbs
1 teaspoon salt
¼ teaspoon pepper
¼ cup butter
1 cup hot bouillon or
  veal stock*

Cut meat into serving pieces. Place in heavy saucepan and cover with boiling water. Add salt. Bring to a boil; skim as often as needed. Reduce heat. Simmer, covered, 1 hour or until meat is tender. Drain; reserve stock. Dry meat with paper towels and remove meat from bones. Trim pieces; brush with egg white. Combine bread crumbs with salt and pepper. Coat meat pieces with bread crumbs. Heat butter and fry meat until golden crisp. Transfer to hot serving dish and keep hot. Stir bouillon into pan and blend with drippings. Boil until the right consistency for sauce has been obtained. Serve meat with green peas and fried potatoes and serve gravy on the side.

Swedish Veal Cutlet à la Oscar

5 TO 6 SERVINGS

This combination of the tenderest veal, lobster, asparagus, and béarnaise sauce is a specialty of first-class Scandinavian restau-

rants. This particular version comes from the luxurious Kron-
prinsen Restaurant in Malmö, where the cuisine ranks with the
finest in Europe, both as to preparation and service.

The asparagus used in Sweden is snow white and very tender. This kind of asparagus can be bought here in specialty stores.

*2½ pounds boneless rump
    of veal, ¾ inch thick
1 teaspoon salt
¼ teaspoon white pepper
¼ cup butter
20 stalks hot cooked
    asparagus, tender
    part only*

*1 ½ cups hot cooked
    lobster meat, diced
Béarnaise Sauce
    (recipe below)
Parsley sprigs*

Cut meat in 5 or 6 serving pieces and trim away all fat and
gristle. Rub meat with salt and pepper. Melt butter in large
skillet. Over medium heat, cook meat until golden on both sides.
Reduce heat, and simmer, covered, about 10 to 15 minutes or
until meat is tender and cooked through. Arrange meat on hot
serving platter. Place 2 asparagus spears on each side of each
round. Fill center with lobster. Cover with béarnaise sauce and
decorate with parsley sprigs. Serve with browned potatoes and
a tossed green salad.

Béarnaise Sauce
MAKES 1½ CUPS

Béarnaise is made like hollandaise sauce. The difference between
the two sauces is that béarnaise is flavored with wine, vinegar,
shallots, pepper, and tarragon, whereas hollandaise is flavored
with lemon juice.

¼ cup wine vinegar	Pinch of salt
¼ cup dry white wine	3 egg yolks
1 tablespoon minced shallots or green onions	2 tablespoons cold butter
½ tablespoon dried tarragon	⅔ cup melted butter
⅛ teaspoon white pepper	1 tablespoon minced parsley

In small saucepan boil together vinegar, wine, shallots, tarragon, pepper, and salt until the liquid has been reduced to 2 tablespoons. Strain; cool to lukewarm. Add egg yolks and beat briskly with a wire whip. Place saucepan over lowest possible heat. Add 1 tablespoon of the cold butter and beat into sauce. Beat in remaining tablespoon of cold butter. Then beat in melted butter, drop by drop, until sauce thickens. Stir in minced parsley.

Swedish Braised Beef Roll

Oxrulader

3 TO 4 SERVINGS

The Swedish version of a dish that is universally popular in all of Scandinavia. The secret is to use lean, well-flavored bacon, such as imported Danish bacon or hickory-smoked bacon.

2 pounds round steak, cut ¼ inch thick	8 slices bacon, about ¼ inch thick
¼ teaspoon pepper	Flour
2 teaspoons prepared mustard	3 tablespoons butter
½ cup minced parsley	½ cup bouillon, hot
	¼ cup heavy cream

Pound meat as thin as possible without breaking it. Use meat mallet or rolling pin. Cut into 8 strips about 4 inches long and 2 inches wide. Season on one side with pepper and spread thinly with mustard and parsley. Place one slice of bacon on the mustard side of each strip of meat. Roll up and secure rolls with toothpicks or small skewers. Coat rolls with flour. Heat butter in heavy skillet. Brown beef rolls on all sides. Add hot bouillon. Simmer, covered, over low heat ¾ to 1 hour, or until meat is tender. Place beef rolls in hot serving dish and keep hot. Add cream to pan juices, scraping bottom of the pan and stirring constantly. Pour over beef rolls and serve with any kind of potatoes and a green vegetable.

Scandinavian Veal Pot Roast

Kalvestek

6 SERVINGS

This is the standard way of making a veal roast in all of Scandinavia. Veal is a delicacy, and cooked this way, it will remain juicy.

4 to 5 pounds veal roast (rump or leg)	3 tablespoons butter
2 teaspoons salt	½ cup bouillon
½ teaspoon ground allspice	2 carrots, sliced
¼ teaspoon pepper	2 onions, sliced
	Heavy cream

Make sure that the meat has not been larded by the butcher. If so, remove sheets of fat. Rub meat on all sides with salt, allspice, and pepper. In heavy casserole or Dutch oven brown meat on all sides in hot butter. Lift meat with a fork, and pour bouillon, carrots and onions into casserole. Place meat on vegetables. Cover tightly. Simmer about 1½ to 2 hours, or until meat is tender. Remove meat to hot platter, slice, and keep hot. Make cream gravy in the usual manner, using heavy cream instead of milk. Or, for a different gravy, purée vegetables and pan drippings in blender. Dilute to proper consistency with heated heavy cream. Heat through but do not boil. Serve gravy separately. Serve meat with browned potatoes and vegetables, arranged decoratively around meat slices.

Danish Veal Patties

Kalve Frikadeller

2 TO 3 SERVINGS

In Denmark the meatball reigns supreme. And good and inexpensive food it is, too.

1 ½ pounds ground veal
½ cup butter, melted
1 teaspoon grated lemon
* rind*
1 ½ teaspoons salt
½ teaspoon white pepper
2 tablespoons plain
* soda water (this*
* gives lightness)*

1 egg, beaten
1 cup dry
* bread crumbs*
2 tablespoons butter
1 cup sweet or
* sour cream*

Combine veal, melted butter, grated lemon rind, salt, and pepper. Stir in soda water. Shape quickly into patties. Dip patties into beaten egg and bread crumbs. Heat butter and cook patties in it about 10 to 15 minutes, depending on size of patties. Turn once. Transfer cooked patties to hot serving dish; keep hot. Stir cream into skillet and heat thoroughly. Pour over patties. Serve in the Danish manner with plain boiled potatoes and cucumber salad.

Swedish Jellied Veal Loaf

16 SERVINGS

No smorgasbord is complete without jellied veal, and there are a great many recipes for it. Most of them would be too bland for our American tastes, since Scandinavians like bland foods. The following recipe makes a well-flavored loaf that holds together without gelatin and keeps in the refrigerator for 4 to 5 days.

1 meaty veal shank (about 2 pounds)	4 bay leaves
2 ¼ pounds veal shoulder	4 whole allspice or ½ teaspoon
1 ¼ pounds lean pork	ground allspice
2 quarts water	½ teaspoon pepper
1 large onion, sliced	Lettuce
2 tablespoons salt	

Place veal shank and meats into deep kettle. Cover with water and add all other ingredients except lettuce. Bring to boiling point. Skim and simmer, covered, over lowest possible heat until meat is very tender. This will take about 2 to 2½ hours. Drain meat and reserve. Strain broth. Simmer broth, uncovered, until reduced to 7 cups liquid. Cool and chill in refrigerator. Remove every trace of fat from top of chilled broth. While broth is chilling, cut meats into ¼-inch cubes or push through medium blade of meat grinder. Return meat to skimmed broth and bring to boiling point. Cook, uncovered, 3 minutes. Pour meat into 3-quart mold or loaf pans. Chill overnight until firm. Unmold on bed of lettuce. Serve with pickled beets.

Swedish Roast Leg of Lamb

Lammstek

6 SERVINGS

The coffee, provided it is not overly strong, gives an excellent color to the meat and a subtle taste to the gravy.

One 5-pound leg of lamb
1 tablespoon salt
1 tablespoon pepper
2 medium-size onions, sliced
2 medium-size carrots, sliced

1 cup bouillon, hot
1 ½ cups coffee, hot
½ cup heavy cream
2 teaspoons sugar
Parsley sprigs
Broiled tomatoes

Set oven at 450°.

Trim lamb of all excess fat. Rub salt and pepper into the meat. Place meat on a rack in a roasting pan and roast 30 minutes. Pour off fat or remove with baster. Reduce oven heat to moderate (350°) and place onions and carrots in the pan. Combine bouillon, coffee, cream, and sugar and pour over meat. Continue roasting for 1 to 1½ hours, depending on the degree of doneness desired. Baste very frequently. Transfer lamb to warm serving platter and keep hot. Strain gravy and press vegetables through a sieve or purée in a blender. Garnish lamb with parsley and broiled tomatoes. Serve with browned potatoes and a green vegetable. Serve sauce separately.

Swedish Boiled Lamb with Dill and Dill Sauce

Kokt Lamm med Dillsås

3 TO 4 SERVINGS

This very popular and excellent dish must be made with fresh dill, which can now be bought all the year round in many American markets.

3 *pounds breast or shoulder of lamb*	4 *white peppercorns*
Boiling water	1 *bay leaf*
1 *tablespoon salt to every quart of water*	5 *dill sprigs*

Trim meat of excess fat and scald quickly in boiling water. Drain, place in casserole or Dutch oven, and add boiling salt water to cover. Bring to a boil and skim. Add remaining ingredients. Simmer, covered, 1 to 1½ hours or until meat is tender. Drain and reserve stock. Cut meat in serving pieces. Place on hot platter and garnish with more dill sprigs. Serve with dill sauce (recipe below) and boiled potatoes.

Dill Sauce

2 *tablespoons butter*	1 ½ *tablespoons white vinegar*
2 *tablespoons flour*	2 *tablespoons sugar*
1 ½ *to 2 cups stock from lamb*	*Salt to taste*
2 *tablespoons chopped dill*	1 *egg yolk, beaten*

Melt butter, add flour, and stir until smooth. Add hot stock gradually, and cook until mixture is thickened and smooth. Simmer, covered, 10 minutes, stirring frequently. Add dill, vinegar, sugar, and salt to taste. Remove from heat and stir in beaten egg yolk. Serve hot.

Roast Lamb à la Kramer

6 SERVINGS

This was the *pièce de résistance* of a perfect Swedish spring dinner served to me at the Hotel Kramer in Malmö. Arthur Kristensson, the *maître*, composed it, beginning with salmon and toast, and continuing with roast lamb and new vegetables and strawberries and cream. We drank a 1955 Château Fonroque, sherry, and Swedish punsch.

One 5-pound leg of lamb, trimmed
1 ½ tablespoons salt
½ tablespoon white pepper
1 lemon, cut in half

¼ cup butter
½ cup fine dry white bread crumbs
2 tablespoons minced parsley
Parsley sprigs

Set oven at 300°.

Rub lamb with salt and pepper and the lemon halves. Place on rack in roasting pan and roast, uncovered, 12 minutes per pound for rare or 18 minutes per pound for well done. Carve lamb in the usual manner, but do not cut the slices off the bone—they must remain attached. Keep hot. Melt butter and brown bread crumbs in it. Stir in parsley. Spread mixture over lamb.

Turn oven to hot (450°) and continue roasting for about 10 minutes, or until topping is crisp. Transfer to serving platter and decorate with parsley. Serve surrounded by rows of buttered baby carrots, small bundles of asparagus tips, small mounds of coarsely chopped buttered spinach, whole mushroom caps sautéed in butter, and small grilled tomatoes.

Norwegian Lamb and Cabbage

Får i Kål

4 TO 5 SERVINGS

The national meat dish of Norway. Norwegian lamb is excellent, since it grazes on the grass of salt marshes, like the prized *pré salé* lamb of France.

4 pounds lamb (any cut, but inexpensive cuts will do)
1 firm medium-size cabbage
1 celery knob or 1 cup diced celery

1½ tablespoons salt
⅓ cup flour
Boiling bouillon or water
2 tablespoons black peppercorns tied in a cheesecloth bag

Trim lamb of excess fat and cut in 2- to 3-inch serving pieces. Core and cut cabbage into 1-inch wedges. Peel celery knob and dice. In heavy saucepan or Dutch oven place a layer of meat, fatty side down. Top with cabbage and sprinkle with some of the celery knob, salt, and flour. Repeat process; there should be at least 3 layers of meat and vegetables. Add bouillon to cover lamb and cabbage halfway. Add bag with peppercorns. Cover tightly and bring to a slow boil. Check occasionally; if necessary, add a little more bouillon. Cook over low heat until meat is tender, about 1½ to 2½ hours. Remove bag with peppercorns before serving. Serve with boiled potatoes.

NOTE: For a richer dish, stir in ½ cup sour cream before serving.

Norwegian Spiced Ribs of Mutton

Bergen Pinnekjøtt

This is another Norwegian national dish and a specialty of the west coast at Christmas time. Americans are not very likely to make it, but in case one of my readers should be seized with the desire, here is the recipe, both the original method and the modernized version.

TRADITIONAL METHOD

Salt a rack of mutton as described in recipe for cured leg of mutton below. Dry in a drafty place for about 3 weeks. To cook, cut between the rib bones for single pieces. Soak meat in cold water for 3 hours. In a large kettle, make a rack of birch twigs. Take twigs a little longer than the diameter of the kettle and press down to make a platform about 1 to 2 inches above the bottom of the kettle. Fill with cold water to the level of the twigs. Place strips of meat on twigs. Cover tightly. Steam about 2 hours. Check for drying out from time to time, and, if necessary, add more water to keep up level. Serve with mashed potatoes and mashed yellow turnips.

NOTE: The birch twigs give *pinnekjøtt* its typical taste.

MODERN VERSION

3 TO 4 SERVINGS

---

2 pounds ribs of mutton
2 tablespoons salt
1 tablespoon sugar

1 to 2 teaspoons
  pepper
2 cups boiling water,
  or more

Trim meat. Combine salt, sugar, and pepper and rub into meat. Dry in drafty place for 3 days. Set oven at 450°. Cut meat into strips. Place in roasting pan and brown in hot oven for 15 minutes. Pour boiling water over ribs. Reduce oven heat to 350°. Cook ribs about 1¾ hours, basting every 10 minutes with pan drippings and more boiling water, if needed. If ribs are drying out, cover with buttered foil or nonwaxed paper.

Norwegian Cured Leg of Mutton

Fenalår

16 TO 20 SERVINGS

This is one of the world's best cold cuts, and is really out of this world. No visitor to Norway should neglect to demand it. The mutton is first cured and then dried for months in the pure fresh Norwegian air. The air is an essential ingredient to make *fenalår*. If you live in one of our cooler states and have access to a leg of mutton (not lamb), try making *fenalår*. The following recipe is a standard one.

In Norway *fenalår* is prepared in September when the sheep are fat after their summer pasture. It is eaten in May,

June, or July. As you travel through the countryside, you see the legs of mutton hanging in drafty spots at the back of the barns.

One 8- to 9-pound leg of mutton	2 pounds salt
¼ cup Cognac	½ cup molasses
1 teaspoon saltpeter (from the drugstore)	1 cup water

Trim meat and rub thoroughly with Cognac. Combine all other ingredients and spread over meat. Place meat in deep stone container and leave in brine for 1 week. Turn several times. Drain and dry meat. Repeat with new brine, soaking for 1 week. Smoke and hang meat.

Brine

1 gallon water	1 tablespoon saltpeter
4 pounds coarse salt	(from the
1 pound sugar	drugstore)

Combine all ingredients and bring to a boil. Cool. Place meat in brine for 1 week. Drain, dry, and smoke lightly. Hang in drafty place for curing—at least 4 months. The meat should shrink to about half the original weight. To serve, cut in wafer-thin slices and remove the outer edge of the fat. Serve on sandwiches, with fried eggs, or as a main dish with spring vegetables and potatoes and melted butter. *Fenalår* may also be cured for 2 months only; then it is cooked like a ham and eaten hot.

Aune's Pork Casserole

5 TO 6 SERVINGS

Aune Merikallio is a Finnish home economist who works in this country but still eats in the Finnish way at home. This pork, sauerkraut, apple, and potato combination makes an excellent main course for a cold day.

*One 4- to 5-pound fresh
  pork shoulder*
2 teaspoons salt
½ teaspoon pepper
*2 teaspoons prepared
  mustard*
*3 cups drained
  sauerkraut*

*3 medium-size apples,
  pared, cored and
  sliced*
1 tablespoon sugar
*4 medium-size potatoes,
  peeled and sliced*

Set oven at 350°.

Trim meat of excess fat. Rub on all sides with salt and pepper and spread with mustard. Place meat on rack in roasting pan. Roast for 1 hour; drain off fat. Remove meat and rack from pan. In the roasting pan now make a layer of sauerkraut. Place apples on sauerkraut and sprinkle with sugar. Top with potatoes. Replace meat in pan on top of potatoes. Cover pan with lid or with foil. Return to oven and bake for 1½ to 2 hours longer or until meat is cooked. During cooking time baste meat several times with pan juices. Serve with pickled beets.

NOTE: This dish can also be made on top of the stove, in a deep kettle. The procedure is the same.

Norwegian Pork Roast Piquant

Svinekam Piquant

4 TO 6 SERVINGS

This excellent roast comes from Derek Blix, who managed the Pan American office in Oslo and helped writers in distress, like this one.

¼ cup Dijon-type
  prepared mustard
1 tablespoon prepared
  horseradish
1 teaspoon anchovy paste
1 tablespoon sugar

1 pork loin, about
  3 to 4 pounds
⅔ cup fine dry
  bread crumbs
2 cups boiling dry
  white wine or water

Set oven at 325°.

Combine mustard, horseradish, anchovy paste, and sugar, and blend to a smooth paste. Trim excess fat off meat. With a brush, spread meat on all sides with mixture. Place on rack in baking pan. Cover top and sides with bread crumbs. Roast 35 to 40 minutes to the pound, or until meat thermometer registers 185°. After 1 hour of roasting time, pour 1 cup boiling wine or water into pan. Be careful that the wine or water does not touch the meat. When the liquid has evaporated completely, pour remaining wine or water into pan. Serve on a platter surrounded by alternating mounds of tiny buttered peas, carrots, and small browned potatoes.

Scandinavian Pork Tenderloin with Prunes

4 SERVINGS

A favorite in the North. This looks well carved, the dark prunes showing against the lighter meat.

12 large prunes
1 ½ to 2 pounds pork
* tenderloin, in one piece*
1 teaspoon salt
½ teaspoon pepper

½ teaspoon ground
* ginger*
3 tablespoons butter
1 cup bouillon or
* water, hot*

Soak prunes in hot water until plumped. Drain and dry prunes. With a sharp knife slit prunes and remove pits. Trim excess fat off meat. With a sharp knife cut tenderloin lengthwise about two thirds through. Arrange prunes in a neat row inside tenderloin. Fasten with skewers or tie with string. Rub meat with salt, pepper, and ground ginger. Brown tenderloin on all sides in hot butter. Add hot bouillon or water. Simmer, covered, over low heat, about 1½ hours or until meat is tender. Baste occasionally; if necessary, add a little more hot bouillon. To serve, carefully remove skewers or string. Make gravy by straining and skimming pan juices and pouring over meat. Or make cream gravy in the usual manner and serve separately.

Finnish Pork Sauce

Sianlihakastike

3 TO 4 SERVINGS

The standard daily lunch for most Finnish people.

½ pound salt or fresh pork, sliced	1 medium-size onion, chopped
3 tablespoons flour	3 cups water, hot

In hot skillet, brown meat quickly on all sides. It should be crisp. Remove meat and keep hot. Stir flour into pan drippings. Cook until browned, stirring constantly. Add onion and continue cooking until browned. Do not burn. Stir in hot water, a little at a time. Cook until sauce is thickened and smooth. Return meat to sauce. Check for seasoning; salt is needed when fresh pork is used. Cook over lowest possible heat about 30 minutes, stirring occasionally. Serve hot with boiled potatoes.

NOTE: Sometimes, the sauce is seasoned to taste with mustard, or paprika, or tomato purée. Or a little cream may be added to it.

Danish Pork Stew with Prunes

3 TO 4 SERVINGS

16 dried prunes	¼ teaspoon ground ginger
Water	
4 pounds pork, with bone (any cut)	3 tablespoons butter or margarine
½ cup flour	½ cup sherry or Madeira
1 ½ teaspoons salt	
½ teaspoon pepper	⅓ cup heavy cream

Plump prunes in water until soft. Drain and dry. Trim pork of excess fat and cut into serving pieces. Combine flour with salt, pepper, and ginger. Dredge pork pieces with flour. Heat butter in heavy saucepan or casserole and brown pork in it on all sides. Pour off most of the fat. Add prunes and sherry or Madeira. Cook, covered, over low heat for 1½ hours or until pork is tender. If necessary, add a little hot water. Transfer meat to hot serving dish and keep hot. Stir cream into pan juices and simmer 1 minute. Pour over meat. Serve with boiled potatoes and a green salad.

NOTE: Instead of 4 pounds of pork with bone, use 2 to 2½ pounds of boneless pork.

Danish Pork Frikadeller

3 TO 4 SERVINGS

All the Norse love meatballs, but the Danes' affection and use for them amounts to a national passion. *Frikadeller* are made from every kind of meat. They are eaten continually, either hot or cold. The club soda makes them light.

2 pounds lean pork, ground fine	1 teaspoon salt
½ cup flour	½ teaspoon pepper
1 egg	½ cup club soda or water
1 tablespoon grated onion	4 tablespoons butter
1 teaspoon grated lemon rind	½ to ¾ cup light or heavy cream

Combine pork, flour, egg, onion, lemon rind, salt, and pepper. Blend thoroughly. Stir in club soda gently. Shape meat into small balls, using hands. Heat butter in skillet. Brown pork balls on all sides. Lower heat and cook about 20 minutes or until done. Transfer pork balls to hot serving dish and keep hot. Add cream to pan juices. Bring to a quick boil, stirring constantly. Pour over pork balls. Serve with boiled or browned potatoes and pickled beets.

NOTE: If *frikadeller* are to be served cold, omit gravy.

Danish Cooked Ham in Madeira Sauce

Kogt Skinke med Madeira

4 TO 6 SERVINGS

From the Rødvig Kro, a charming old inn in south Zealand.

One 2-pound canned
Danish ham

⅓ cup dark brown sugar
2 tablespoons Madeira

Set oven at 350°.
  Remove ham from can and remove gelatin coating. Make a paste of brown sugar and Madeira. Spread paste over ham. Bake for 30 minutes. Slice and serve with Madeira sauce (recipe below).

Madeira Sauce

¼ cup butter
2 tablespoons grated
  onion or 1 teaspoon
  instant onion powder
¼ cup flour

2 cups brown stock or
  beef bouillon, hot
⅓ cup Madeira
½ teaspoon salt
¼ teaspoon pepper

Melt butter. Stir in onion and cook over low heat 2 minutes. Stir in flour. Gradually add hot brown stock or beef bouillon. Cook over low heat until sauce is thick and smooth, stirring constantly. Add Madeira and salt and pepper. Reheat, but do not boil. Serve hot over sliced ham.

Madeira Sauce for Tongue

Tongue, cooked in the usual manner, is a Danish favorite, both hot and cold. Sauce is often served with it.

Plump ¼ cup yellow raisins in hot water. Drain; add the hot raisins to Madeira sauce (see above) before adding the wine and seasonings. Proceed as above.

SWEDISH CHRISTMAS HAM

Part of the traditional Christmas Eve supper in Sweden, but very good all the year round. The following recipe begins with the curing of the ham, but a cured one can also be used for baking, though not quite as satisfactorily. Allow about 3½ weeks for a home-cured ham.

TO CURE HAM

*One 10- to 12-pound
  fresh ham
1 cup salt
¼ cup sugar*

*2 teaspoons saltpeter
  (from the
  drugstore)*

Prepare a large stone crock or a deep enamel pan. Do not use aluminum. Combine 1 cup salt, ¼ cup sugar, and 2 teaspoons saltpeter. Wipe fresh ham with a cloth. Rub salt mixture into the ham on all sides. Sprinkle any remaining salt mixture over ham. Place ham in crock. Let stand in a cool place or refrigerator for 3 days.

TO CURE HAM IN BRINE

3 cups salt
½ cup brown sugar
1 tablespoon saltpeter
  (from the drugstore)
2 teaspoons whole
  cloves
4 to 5 quarts boiling
  water

Add salt, sugar, saltpeter, and cloves to boiling water. Boil for 2 minutes. Cool. Pour brine over ham in crock. (Do *not* remove the previous salt mixture from ham.) The ham should be completely covered by the brine. Place a plate weighted with some canned goods or other heavy objects on ham to keep it down in the brine. Cover crock. Let ham stand for 3 weeks.

TO COOK HAM

Boiling water
3 bay leaves
12 whole peppercorns
12 whole allspice
1 medium-size onion

Remove ham from brine and drain thoroughly. Place ham in deep kettle and cover with boiling water, bay leaves, whole pepper, allspice, and onion. Cover kettle. Simmer ham until tender, about 4 to 5 hours. Do not boil ham, but keep liquid just at simmering point, not more. Remove ham from heat and let cool in liquid. Drain cooled ham. Trim off skin and excess fat. Place ham on rack in roasting pan.

TO GLAZE HAM

2 egg whites
2 tablespoons sugar
2 tablespoons dry
mustard

⅓ cup fine dry
bread crumbs

Set oven at 350°.

Beat egg whites until they stand in soft peaks. Beat in sugar and mustard. Brush mixture over ham, fat side up, and cover well on all sides. Cover thinly but evenly with bread crumbs. Bake ham 35 to 45 minutes or until glaze is brown. Remove ham to platter.

TO GARNISH HAM

Paper frills
Parsley sprigs

Soft butter
(optional)

Garnish bone of ham with a paper frill and surround with parsley sprigs. If the ham is to be served cold, fill smallest pastry tube with softened butter and pipe decorative swirls and loops on ham. You might also write on it: *God Jul*, that is, Merry Christmas!

Ham Leftovers with Madeira Sauce

4 SERVINGS

---

6 slices Danish ham
1 tablespoon butter
1 tablespoon flour
1 teaspoon tomato paste

¾ cup Madeira
⅔ cup heavy cream
Salt and pepper to
taste

Set oven at 350°.

Remove ham from refrigerator while preparing sauce. Butter a shallow ovenproof dish and warm slightly. Arrange ham slices in it so that they overlap somewhat. Melt butter and stir in flour and tomato paste. Add Madeira and cook over low heat until mixture thickens, stirring constantly. Remove from heat, and slowly add the heavy cream. Season with salt and pepper. Pour sauce over ham and bake 10 minutes or until ham is heated through.

NOTE: If your ham leftovers do not make presentable slices, cut the ham into cubes or strips, and serve the dish over hot buttered toast, rice or noodles.

Canned Danish Pork Loin with Quick Currant Sauce

2 TO 4 SERVINGS

Canned Danish pork loin, imported into this country, resembles Canadian bacon, though it is more full-flavored.

1 small canned Danish
pork loin, thickly sliced
(about 1 pound)
¼ cup butter
3 tablespoons red
currant jelly

1 to 2 teaspoons
prepared mustard
1 teaspoon grated
onion or ½
teaspoon instant
onion

Brown pork loin slices in butter on all sides. Remove to hot platter; keep hot. Into the skillet in which the pork loin was browned stir red currant jelly, mustard, and onion. Blend thoroughly and heat through, but do not boil. Pour over pork loin slices and serve with browned potatoes.

Danish Bacon and Potatoes

Braendende Kaerlighed

A very simple and remarkably good Danish family dish. For best results, use the readily available (in U.S.A. supermarkets) canned smoked Danish pork loin, which is excellent, or Canadian-style bacon.

Cut as many slices of bacon as you'll need. Fry them and keep them hot. Pile very hot and very rich mashed potatoes on a flat serving dish in the shape of a pyramid. Surround with fried bacon slices. Garnish with parsley and serve with pickled beets on the side.

Swedish Hash

Pytt i Panna

4 SERVINGS

Simple, nourishing, and good.

6 tablespoons butter	Salt and pepper
3 medium-size onions,	to taste
diced	Fried eggs
3 cups diced, peeled	Cucumber pickles,
boiled potatoes	sliced
3 cups diced leftover	
meat	

Heat 2 tablespoons of the butter and cook onions in it until soft and golden. Transfer to hot plate. Brown potatoes in 2 tablespoons butter and transfer to hot plate. Brown meat in remaining butter. Return onions and potatoes to skillet and mix thoroughly with meat. Season with salt and pepper and heat through. Arrange on hot platter and garnish with fried eggs (one for each serving) and sliced cucumber pickles.

Norwegian Brown Hash

Brun Lapskaus

4 SERVINGS

A standard Scandinavian way of using up leftovers. This particular version comes from Doris Løkke of Bodø in northern

Norway, well above the Arctic Circle. Doris, a Swiss girl, married a Norwegian in Brazil. After living on a farm in a remote Norwegian valley, where things had not changed for a hundred years, she ran the Bodø Tourist Office with great efficiency.

3 cups chopped cold roast
   pork or ham or beef
3 cups chopped cold
   peeled boiled potatoes
⅓ cup butter or
   margarine
2 medium-size onions,
   sliced

1 ½ teaspoons salt
½ teaspoon pepper
1 cup boiling
   bouillon, or more
¼ cup sherry
   (optional)

Brown meat and potataoes in hot butter. Add onions, salt, and pepper. Add boiling bouillon to cover. Bring to a boil; reduce heat. Cover and simmer over low heat about 45 minutes, stirring occasionally. If necessary, add a little more boiling bouillon, one tablespoon at a time. All the bouillon must be absorbed in the finished dish. Stir in sherry. Serve very hot, with parsleyed steamed potatoes and cucumber salad.

Danish Hash

Hachis

2 TO 3 SERVINGS

Meat is so much more expensive in Scandinavia than in the United States that the thrifty housewives of these countries have learned the art of good leftover dishes like this one.

2 ½ cups leftover
　roast or boiled
　beef or pork
2 medium-size onions,
　chopped
¼ cup butter
¼ cup flour
1 ½ cups beef bouillon

½ cup red wine
1 teaspoon Kitchen
　Bouquet
¼ cup pickle relish
½ teaspoon salt
6 fried eggs
12 small sugar-
　browned potatoes

Grind meat fine. Cook onions in hot butter until soft and golden. Stir in flour. Gradually stir in the beef bouillon and red wine. Cook over low heat until smooth and thick, stirring constantly. Stir in Kitchen Bouquet, pickle relish, salt, and ground meat. Heat through thoroughly. Serve hot topped with fried eggs and sugar-browned potatoes.

Swedish Meatballs

Köttbullar

4 SERVINGS

The dish that made Swedish cooking beloved to Americans. Small, they are for the smorgasbord; bigger for an entrée; when served as entrée, they must have their cream gravy in the Swedish manner.

There are probably as many ways of making Swedish meatballs as there are Swedish housewives. They can be made from one kind of meat only, but I think that a combination gives a better flavor. Whatever the ingredients, the meatballs must be light and should not be handled too much.

2 tablespoons butter
¼ cup finely chopped
  onion
½ to ⅔ cup fine dry
  bread crumbs
¾ cup light cream
¾ pound ground round
  steak
¼ pound ground veal

¼ pound ground
  lean pork
2 teaspoons salt
¼ teaspoon pepper
⅛ teaspoon ground
  cloves
⅓ cup butter
¼ cup boiling water

Heat butter and sauté onion in it until soft and golden. Soak bread crumbs in cream. Combine onion, bread crumbs, meats, salt, pepper, and cloves and blend thoroughly, but with a light hand. Shape mixture with hands into small balls. Wet hands so that meat will not stick. Heat butter and fry meatballs until brown on all sides, shaking pan continuously to prevent sticking. Add boiling water and simmer over lowest possible heat for 5 minutes longer. For the smorgasbord serve on toothpicks. For an entrée make larger meatballs, and make cream gravy as usual with pan juices.

Finnish Karelian "Hotpot"

Karjalan Paisti

4 TO 6 SERVINGS

A typical Finnish meat dish, which must be made with the three different kinds of meat or it won't be right. The flavors combine very well, provided the dish is baked extremely slowly. In Finnish country homes the "hotpot" is often left overnight in the residual heat of the oven after the baking of bread.

1 pound lean pork	*½ teaspoon ground*
1 pound beef round	*allspice*
1 pound boned lamb	*6 medium-size onions,*
2 teaspoons salt	*sliced*
½ teaspoon pepper	*Bouillon or water,*
	hot

Set oven at 350°.

Cut meats into 2-inch cubes. Sprinkle with salt, pepper, and allspice. Arrange alternate layers of meats and onions in deep casserole or baking dish. Add just enough hot bouillon or water to cover meats. Cover and bake about 3 hours, or until meats are fork-tender. Check occasionally for moisture; if necessary, add a little more hot bouillon. The dish should have some, but not too much, pan juice. Serve with boiled or baked potatoes.

Finnish Liver Casserole

3 TO 4 SERVINGS

Liver is a favorite in all Scandinavian countries, and it is cooked with far more imagination and taste than in America. This Finnish liver casserole is excellent, and even non-liver-eaters will like it.

½ cup butter, melted	*3 cups cooked rice*
1 medium-size onion,	*¾ cup dark corn*
chopped	*syrup*
2 eggs	*½ cup raisins*
3 cups milk	*1 tablespoon salt*
1 ½ pounds beef	
liver, ground raw	

Set oven at 400°.

Pour 2 tablespoons melted butter into skillet. Add onion and cook over low heat until soft and translucent. Beat eggs in large bowl until foamy. Blend in milk. Mix in cooked onion and remaining ingredients. Pour into buttered 3-quart casserole. Bake about 1½ hours or until firm. Serve with lingonberry sauce or cranberry catsup.

Swedish Liver Pâté

Lefverpastej

4 SERVINGS

The anchovies give this liver pâté the characteristic Swedish touch.

1 pound beef liver	1 slice white bread
Milk	1 egg, well beaten
2 medium-size onions	3 tablespoons flour
½ pound salt pork	½ teaspoon pepper
6 anchovy fillets, drained	6 slices bacon

Soak liver in milk to cover for 4 hours. Drain and dry. Grind liver with onions twice. Grind salt pork, anchovies, and bread twice. Combine liver and salt pork mixtures. Add ½ cup milk, egg, flour, and pepper. Blend thoroughly. Line an 8½- by 4½-inch loaf pan with bacon slices. Press liver mixture firmly into pan. Bake in moderate oven (350°) 1 hour. Cover top to prevent overbrowning. Cool before unmolding. Chill before serving.

Norwegian Kidneys in White Wine

Nyrer i Hvitvin

3 TO 4 SERVINGS

---

4 veal kidneys
¼ cup butter
1 tablespoon chopped
    parsley
½ pound mushrooms,
    sliced thin

2 tablespoons flour
1 cup dry white wine
½ cup bouillon,
    or more
Salt and pepper to
    taste

Trim kidneys and cut into thin slices. Place in cold water and let stand half an hour, changing water twice. Drain and wipe kidneys dry. Heat butter in skillet, and brown kidneys rapidly on all sides. Sprinkle with parsley and add mushrooms. Cook 1 minute, stirring constantly. Sprinkle with flour and add white wine and bouillon. Cook over medium heat 5 minutes, stirring all the time. If too thick, add a little more bouillon. Season with salt and pepper to taste. Serve very hot, with steamed potatoes.

REINDEER MEAT

Reindeer for meat are raised by the nomad Lapps of northern Norway, and the meat is sold throughout the country either fresh or frozen. Like venison, the meat is dark, lean, and tangy. It is usually marinated before cooking. Any venison recipe can be used for reindeer meat.

The following recipe comes from the Grand Hotel in Tromsø, the capital of northern Norway and an important cultural, fishing, and sporting center. It is also the starting point for Arctic expeditions. The Grand Hotel is as comfortable as any good American hotel, with excellent food and dancing every night—as in most Norwegian hotels. When I was there, an old Lapp woman brought a whole reindeer and skinned and cut it up in no time, while squatting in the hotel yard.

Reindeer Pot Roast with Mushrooms, Tomatoes, Grapes, and Pineapple

Reinsdyrmedaljong med Champignons, Tomat, Druer og Ananas

6 SERVINGS

One 5-pound roast of
  reindeer, boned
  and rolled
1 quart dry red wine
1 large onion, sliced
1 stalk celery
10 peppercorns
1 tablespoon salt

2 bay leaves
½ pound salt pork or
  bacon, cut in slices
½ cup butter
1 cup sour cream
Flour (optional)
½ cup heavy cream,
  whipped

GARNISH

1 pound mushroom
  caps, sautéed in butter
6 tomatoes, cut in half
  and grilled

½ pound dark blue
  grapes, stemmed
1 cup chopped
  pineapple,
  sautéed in butter

Place meat in deep bowl. Combine wine, onion, celery, pepper-corns, salt, and bay leaves. Boil first. Pour over meat and marinate for 24 to 48 hours. Turn meat several times. Drain and wipe dry. Strain marinade and reserve.

Lard meat with salt pork or bacon, or wrap larding around meat, tying with string. Heat butter in large heavy casserole or Dutch oven. Brown meat on all sides. Reduce heat to lowest possible. Pour half of the marinade over meat. Simmer, covered, about 2 to 3 hours (depending on toughness of the meat) or until meat is tender. To test for doneness, lift meat and test with a skewer: it should not draw blood. Baste occasionally during cooking time with pan juices: if necessary, add a little more marinade. When done, transfer meat to hot platter and keep hot. Remove string and salt pork or bacon. Make gravy by swirling sour cream in pan in which meat was cooked, but do not boil. (If necessary, thicken gravy with a little flour mixed with water to a smooth paste. Begin with 1 teaspoon and cook 2 to 3 minutes on lowest possible heat. Slice meat. Add whipped cream to finished gravy and spoon a little over meat on platter. Surround meat with mushroom caps in rows and alternate mounds of grilled tomatoes, grapes, and pineapple. The arrangement should be decorative. Serve remaining gravy separately. Serve with browned potatoes.

WHALE MEAT

Whaling is a major Norwegian industry, carried on in super-modern ships that are floating factories for the processing of the whole animal. Whale meat is readily available throughout Norway, and inexpensive. The meat is dark red and looks like meat, not fish. Properly prepared, it tastes like beef and not like fish. It is important to soak the whale meat several hours (3 hours or more) in iced water to remove any possible fishy taste. Change water several times.

Whale Meat in Brown Sauce

4 SERVINGS

2 pounds whale meat
Iced water
¼ cup flour, or more
1 teaspoon salt
½ teaspoon pepper
¼ cup butter or bacon fat,
   or other fat

2 medium-size onions,
   sliced
1 cup boiling bouillon
   or water, or more
2 bay leaves
½ cup sour cream
   (optional)

Soak whale meat in iced water for at least 3 hours, changing water several times. Drain; dry thoroughly. Cut meat across the grain into 3- or 4-inch square pieces. Pound pieces with meat pounder or rolling pin. (Or sprinkle with meat tenderizer according to directions.) Combine flour, salt, and pepper. Dredge meat pieces with flour mixture. Heat butter and brown onions in it. Push onions to one side of the skillet or casserole, and brown whale meat on all sides. Cover with boiling bouillon or water and add bay leaves. Simmer, covered, for 1 hour or until meat tests tender. Check gravy consistency; thicken, if necessary, with a little more flour. For a richer gravy, stir in ½ cup sour cream.

Whale Meat Cooked Like Venison

4 SERVINGS

2 pounds whale meat
Iced water
½ pound salt pork or
    bacon, cut into thin strips
¼ cup butter
1 cup milk
1 cup water

5 peppercorns
2 bay leaves
1 teaspoon salt
1 teaspoon sugar
⅔ cup sour cream
1 or 2 tablespoons
    flour (optional)

Soak whale meat in iced water for 3 or more hours, changing water several times. Drain; dry thoroughly. Lard meat with salt pork, using larding needle, or make holes in meat with thick knitting needle and push pork strips through the holes. Or wrap strips around meat, tying with string. Brown meat in hot butter on all sides in casserole or Dutch oven. Cover with milk and water. Add peppercorns, bay leaves, salt, and sugar. Cover tightly and simmer about 1 hour or until meat is tender. Turn meat several times during cooking. Place meat on hot serving platter; remove strings and pork. Keep hot. Strain pan juices and stir in sour cream. If a thicker gravy is desired, stir 1 or 2 tablespoons flour moistened with water to a smooth paste into pan juices. Cook for 3 minutes and proceed as above.

More About Whale Meat

After soaking in iced water (see above), whale meat can be prepared as panfried steak, as boneless birds, and ground for patties and meatballs, just like beef. Leftovers can be used in any standard way.

VEGETABLES, BUTTERS, AND SAUCES

---

*T*raditionally, prior to modern refrigeration, the vegetables that could grow in a cold climate and that were easy to store served the Scandinavians as they served all northern people. Except for potatoes, cabbages and root vegetables were plainly cooked in stews, in small quantities. The advent of canning and freezing, especially of vegetables and fruit, changed and enriched this situation to an extent extraordinary to Americans used to today's fine fresh produce, not to mention modern food distribution. I shall always remember that when I first went to Norway, some of the most common canned foods in the United States, such as beans, peaches, and pineapple slices, were considered a delicacy.

Classic Scandinavian cooking has always gone in for mushrooms in a big way. At mushroom time, Norwegians and Finns take off for the woods—or at least they used to—to gather the free bounty of their large forests; Scandinavian mushroom cookery is very good indeed. Besides, mushrooms stand for festive fare, and as a Danish lady told me, if you put mushrooms and cream into a dish, it becomes elegant company eating.

Like all Germanic people, Scandinavians go in for gravies,

especially creamy gravies, compound butters, and simple sauces. Compared to French sauces, Scandinavian traditional gravies are not subtle. But they are much simpler to make, and will invariably appeal to those who have a basic taste for meat, potatoes, and gravies.

Norwegian Cabbage with Sour Cream

3 TO 4 SERVINGS

I had this on the train that took me to Bodø in northern Norway, and it seemed an excellent way to alleviate the dullness of cabbage. By the way, Norwegian trains are very cozy and comfortable, both in the way of passengers and personnel. The conductors even announce over the loudspeaker such notable sights as Sigrid Undset's farm!

*1 medium-size cabbage,
    shredded (about
    4 cups)
Water
1 ½ teaspoons salt*

*½ teaspoon pepper
⅔ cup sour cream,
    or more
1 tablespoon dill seeds*

Cook cabbage in just enough water to keep it from burning. Stir frequently. The cabbage should be tender, but still crisp. Stir in salt, pepper, sour cream, and dill seeds. Cook, covered, over lowest possible heat 5 to 10 minutes, stirring frequently to prevent scorching. If necessary, add a little more sour cream.

NOTE: This dish is even better when made with Savoy cabbage.

Swedish, Norwegian Hot Cauliflower with Shrimp

3 TO 4 SERVINGS

This makes a good luncheon entrée.

1 large cauliflower   Boiling salt water

Sauce

2 cups milk
1 thin onion slice or 1
   teaspoon powdered
   onion
2 sprigs dill or parsley
1/4 cup butter
1/4 cup flour
1 teaspoon salt

1/4 teaspoon white
   pepper
2 cups cold cooked
   shelled shrimp,
   chopped or whole
1/4 cup heavy cream,
   whipped
Minced dill or parsley

Trim cauliflower, wash thoroughly, and cook whole in boiling salt water. Meanwhile, make sauce. Combine milk, onion, and dill or parsley sprigs and bring to a boil. Remove dill or parsley. Melt butter, stir in flour, and cook 2 minutes stirring constantly. Do not let brown. Stir hot milk into mixture, stirring all the while. Cook, stirring constantly, until mixture is thickened and smooth. Cook 2 minutes longer. Season with salt and pepper. Add shrimp and cook over lowest possible heat until shrimp are heated through. Fold whipped cream into sauce. Place hot cauliflower on serving dish and pour sauce over it. Sprinkle with minced dill or parsley.

Swedish Cauliflower with Egg Sauce

Blomkål med Ägg

4 SERVINGS

Cauliflower grows well in the Scandinavian latitudes; hence it is a favorite vegetable.

1 large cauliflower
Boiling salt water
¼ cup butter
⅔ cup minced onion
2 tablespoons fine dry
bread crumbs

2 hard-cooked eggs,
chopped fine
¼ cup minced parsley
or dill
1 teaspoon salt
¼ teaspoon pepper

Boil cauliflower whole or broken in flowerets. While it is cooking, make the sauce. Melt butter in skillet and cook onion in it until soft and golden. Stir in bread crumbs, eggs, parsley or dill, and salt and pepper. Toss lightly until blended. Place cauliflower in serving dish and pour sauce over it.

Danish Red Cabbage

Rødkål

4 SERVINGS

Very good and even better if made the day before it is to be served, and then reheated. This is a sweet-sour dish and, according to taste, a little more sugar and vinegar may be added.

3 pounds red cabbage
3 tablespoons butter
1 tablespoon sugar
1 tablespoon cider
   vinegar
½ cup water, or more

½ cup red currant
   jelly
2 apples, peeled,
   cored and chopped
Salt and pepper to
   taste

Remove tough outer leaves and core from cabbage. Shred fine. In heavy saucepan, heat butter and melt sugar. Do not brown. Add cabbage, cook 3 minutes, and add vinegar and water. Simmer, covered, for 2 to 3 hours, or until very tender. Stir occasionally and, if needed to prevent scorching, add a little more hot water. Half an hour before cabbage is done, add red currant jelly, apples, salt and pepper. Continue cooking, stirring occasionally.

Norwegian Cold Cauliflower with Shrimp

4 SERVINGS

This makes an attractive dish for a smorgasbord. From the Hotel Continental in Oslo.

1 large cauliflower
Boiling salt water
1½ cups mayonnaise (or
   more, depending on
   size of cauliflower)

1 pound cold cooked
   shelled shrimp
1 hard-cooked egg,
   sliced
Dill or parsley sprigs

Trim cauliflower, wash thoroughly, and cook whole in boiling salt water. Drain; cool and transfer to serving dish. Spread cauliflower with mayonnaise. Arrange shrimp on it in decorative design. Garnish with hard-cooked egg slices and dill or parsley sprigs.

NOTE: For a festive occasion, the cauliflower may be garnished as elaborately as you like with olives, pimiento strips, tomato slices, etc.

Britt's Stuffed Cauliflower

4 TO 6 SERVINGS

Britt Axelson is a dashing Swedish lady farmer who cooks this for her people. The dish is good family fare and can be made with any favorite meat loaf combination.

2 medium-size cauliflowers
Boiling salt water
1 pound ground meat
  (beef, pork, veal, or
  any combination)
½ cup fine dry
  bread crumbs
¾ cup chopped parsley
1 egg
1 ½ teaspoons salt
½ teaspoon pepper
Dash of hot pepper
  sauce
⅔ cup butter

Set oven at 350°.

Trim cauliflowers of green leaves. Turn upside down, and with sharp knife scoop out main stalk to make cavity. Take care not to break off buds. Wash cauliflowers and cook in boiling salt water until just tender. Combine all other ingredients except butter and blend thoroughly. Line baking dish with aluminum foil and butter heavily with half of the butter. Fill cauliflower cavities with meat mixture. Place on aluminum foil, meat side down. Dot with remaining butter. Cover tightly with more aluminum foil so that cauliflower is completely covered. Bake about 30 to 40 minutes. Place on hot platter and serve with tomato or mushroom or curry sauce.

Finnish Mushroom Cookery

I was introduced to the wonderful world of Finnish mushrooms by Pan American's Paul P. Suni. In all of my gastronomical wanderings, I have never met with such a variety of mushrooms nor tasted better ones. To us, used to one kind of cultivated mushroom, the subtle and different tastes of the various Finnish mushrooms are a revelation.

Mushrooms are part of the standard Finnish diet. They are eaten fresh, and they are smoked and pickled for preservation. During the mushroom season, which begins at the end of August, the Finns, in family groups, go mushrooming in the incredibly beautiful woods that cover a great part of the country. There are over 100 edible mushrooms, all different, all wonderful.

The following recipes are popular ones, and of course, they taste very different depending on the kind of mushroom used.

Finnish Baked Mushrooms à la Suni

3 TO 4 SERVINGS

---

1 pound mushrooms
Lemon juice
2 tablespoons grated
   onion or 1 large
   shallot, minced
½ cup butter
Salt and pepper to taste

2 tablespoons flour
2 cups heavy cream
4 egg yolks, lightly
   beaten
¼ cup fine dry
   bread crumbs

Set oven at 425°.

Trim mushrooms and slice thin. Sprinkle with lemon juice to keep white. Simmer, tightly covered, with onion and ¼ cup butter. Season with salt and pepper and stir in flour. Cook about 3 minutes. Place in buttered 1½-quart or 2-quart baking dish. Beat together cream and egg yolks. Pour mixture over mushrooms. Sprinkle with bread crumbs and dot with remaining ¼ cup butter. Bake 10 minutes or until golden brown.

Finnish Mushrooms with Sour Cream

3 SERVINGS

¼ cup butter
2 tablespoons grated onion or 1 medium-size shallot, sliced thinly
1 pound mushrooms, sliced

1 teaspoon salt
¼ teaspoon white pepper
⅛ teaspoon grated nutmeg
1 cup sour cream

Melt butter and cook onion or shallot in it for 3 minutes. Add mushrooms, salt, pepper, and nutmeg. Cook over medium heat until mushrooms are browned and pan liquid almost evaporated. Remove from heat and stir in sour cream. Heat through again, but do not boil.

Scandinavian Glazed Onions

3 SERVINGS

---

1 pound small white onions, peeled
1 tablespoon sugar
1 teaspoon salt

2 tablespoons butter
1 cup bouillon or water

Place onions in heavy skillet. Sprinkle with sugar and salt. Add butter and bouillon. Simmer until bouillon has been absorbed. Fry in skillet over low heat until onions are golden brown and glazed, shaking pan frequently to avoid sticking. Serve with roast meats.

Madeleine Hamilton's Potato-Mushroom Ragout

4 SERVINGS

From a former Swedish skiing champion who is also an excellent cook.

4 cups hot mashed potatoes	1 pound mushrooms, sliced
2 eggs, beaten	¼ cup butter
1 teaspoon salt	2 tablespoons melted butter
½ teaspoon pepper	
⅛ teaspoon ground cardamom	⅓ cup chopped chives or parsley

Set oven at 425°.

Combine potatoes, eggs, salt, pepper, and cardamom and mix thoroughly. Sauté mushrooms in ¼ cup hot butter until just limp. They must be still firm. Place mushrooms into the bottoms of individual well-buttered baking dishes. Top with a border of mashed potatoes piped through a tube in decorative swirls. Or else, use a fork and score the border with the fork to make a pattern. Paint potatoes with melted butter and sprinkle with chives. Bake until potatoes are slightly browned. Or broil under medium broiler.

NOTE: This dish can also be baked in a shallow baking dish and brought to the table in it.

Norwegian Butter-Steamed New Potatoes

4 TO 6 SERVINGS

Delicious with fresh boiled salmon. I first had this combination at the Grand Hotel in Tromsø, an important and very civilized Norwegian city well above the Arctic Circle.

20 to 24 tiny new potatoes, about 1 inch or less in diameter
6 to 8 tablespoons butter

Salt and pepper
3 tablespoons chopped fresh dill

Scrub potatoes with wire brush, but do not peel. Melt butter in heavy casserole. Add potatoes and season with salt and pepper. Cover casserole tightly so that no steam will escape. Cook over lowest possible heat until potatoes are tender. Shake casserole frequently to prevent sticking. Sprinkle with dill before serving.

Danish Sugar-Browned Potatoes

Brunede Kartofler

3 TO 4 SERVINGS

A favorite Danish way with potatoes.

12 small potatoes
Boiling salt water

¼ cup sugar
¼ cup butter

Cook potatoes in boiling salt water until tender. Drain and peel. Cook sugar in a skillet over low heat until sugar turns brown. Add butter. Stir constantly until smooth. Add potatoes. Roll potatoes in sugar-butter mixture until coated and golden brown. Serve with pork, poultry, ham, and all meats.

Browned Potatoes the Scandinavian Way

4 TO 5 SERVINGS

2 pounds hot boiled
   potatoes (very small
   potatoes are best)
2 tablespoons butter

⅓ cup fine dry
   bread crumbs
1 teaspoon salt
½ teaspoon sugar

Peel potatoes and if necessary shape into small balls. Melt butter in heavy skillet and brown bread crumbs, salt, and sugar in it. Add potatoes and shake continuously until potatoes are covered with bread crumbs and golden brown. Remove from pan and serve piping hot.

Swedish Creamed Potatoes

Skånsk Potatis

4 TO 5 SERVINGS

From southern Sweden, and far better than most creamed potatoes.

6 tablespoons butter
2 medium-size onions,
   sliced thin
6 cups peeled and diced
   raw potatoes
1 ½ teaspoons salt

¼ teaspoon white
   pepper
1 cup light cream,
   or more
3 tablespoons minced
   parsley or dill

Heat 2 tablespoons of the butter in skillet and cook onions in it until soft and golden. Transfer onions to casserole. Heat remaining butter and sauté potatoes in it until golden brown and half cooked. Transfer potatoes to casserole. Season with salt and pepper and mix thoroughly with onions. Add cream. Simmer, covered, over lowest possible heat until potatoes are done, about 15 minutes. The cream should be absorbed, and the potatoes creamy. Stir occasionally and check for dryness; if necessary add more cream, a little at a time. Before serving, sprinkle with parsley or dill.

> NOTE: It is impossible to give accurate amounts for cream. Different kinds of potatoes will absorb different amounts of cream, and the absorption of cream depends also on the shape of the casserole. However, the dish is very easy to make; all it needs is a little attention.

Finnish Rutabaga Pudding

4 TO 5 SERVINGS

An old-time dish served at Christmas with the Christmas ham, and a very good way of using a neglected winter vegetable.

*8 cups peeled and diced
 rutabagas or swedes
Water
1 ½ teaspoons salt
¼ teaspoon pepper
⅛ teaspoon grated
 nutmeg*

*2 teaspoons sugar or
 dark syrup or
 molasses
¼ cup fine dry
 bread crumbs
¼ cup light cream
2 eggs, beaten
¼ cup butter*

Set oven at 375°.

Cook rutabagas in water to cover until soft. Drain but reserve liquid. Mash rutabagas as for mashed potatoes. Beat in reserved liquid, salt, pepper, nutmeg, and sugar. Soak bread crumbs in light cream. Beat eggs into bread crumb mixture. Combine with rutabagas and blend thoroughly. Place in well-buttered baking dish. Smooth surface and dot with butter. Bake about 1 hour or until pudding tests done and is gently browned on top. Serve with meats.

Finnish Karelian Pasties

Karjalan Piiraat

ABOUT 10 PASTIES

Karelian pasties are an old, old Finnish national dish, the substantial food of people who have to work hard outdoors in a cold climate. Though I don't believe that they will be popular in America, I feel they have a place in this book because they are so very unusual, in appearance and in taste, with an air of history, so to speak.

FILLING

1 cup raw rice (do not use converted rice)	1 teaspoon salt
	2 cups milk
2 cups water	3 hard-cooked eggs,
1 tablespoon butter	chopped

PASTRY

---

1 cup water	2 cups all-purpose
1 teaspoon salt	flour
2 cups rye flour	

DIPPING

---

1 cup boiling water	6 tablespoons butter

To make filling: Wash rice under running cold water. Combine 2 cups water, butter, and salt in a saucepan. Bring to a boil and add rice. Cover and simmer until water is absorbed. Add milk. Cover and simmer until milk is absorbed, stirring occasionally. Cook until rice is tender. Fold hard-cooked eggs into rice.

To make pastry: Combine water and salt. Stir in rye flour first and then all-purpose flour. Knead until dough is smooth and elastic. Divide dough into 20 equal parts. On floured board roll out dough into wafer-thin rounds. Place rounds on top of each other, sprinkling a little flour between them to avoid sticking.

To assemble and bake pasties: Place a heaping tablespoon of filling on each pastry round. Spread the filling into an oval shape, from one end of round to the other, leaving the opposite sides uncovered to the width of 1 inch each. Turn in edges and fold uncovered pastry sides over filling. Do not cover filling entirely; leave an uncovered strip about ¼ inch wide. Crimp the edges of each pasty with finger and thumb to resemble pleats.

Set oven at 425°.

Place pasties on greased and floured baking sheets. Bake

about 15 to 20 minutes or until golden. While pasties are baking, make dipping.

To make dipping: Combine water and butter and keep hot. Dip baked pasties into buttered water as soon as they are baked and while still hot. Place dipped pasties on top of each other and cover with a clean kitchen towel. Let stand covered about 15 minutes. Spread with butter and eat while still warm.

NOTE: To store Karelian pasties, wrap them tightly in aluminum foil. To heat, place them in top of double boiler over boiling water, or warm, tightly wrapped, in hot oven (425°) for 3 to 5 minutes. As a variation Karelian pasties can also be filled with mashed potatoes or medium barley. The barley should be cooked in the same fashion as is the rice in the above recipe.

SCANDINAVIAN COMPOUND BUTTERS

These butters are used in all good Scandinavian restaurants with meats, fish, and vegetables. They do a world of good to everyday hamburgers and the eternal broiled chicken, and I recommend their use at home. Compound butters are extremely easy to make, either by hand or in a blender, and they keep well in the refrigerator, provided they're wrapped up tight or covered, as with any butter.

When using a blender, scrape off sides frequently with a rubber spatula, and use the spatula also to guide the ingredients into the processing blades. To all of these butters add salt to taste.

Shape the compound butter into a roll 1 inch in diameter and wrap in aluminum foil or waxed paper. At serving time cut off ½-inch pats (or pats of any desired size) and serve.

Garlic Butter

ABOUT 1 CUP

For French bread, meat, fish, and vegetables.

Cream 1 cup butter and beat in 2 or 3 crushed cloves of garlic. Or add whole garlic cloves to blender while making butter.

Blue Cheese Butter

ABOUT 1¼ CUPS

Cream 1 cup butter and beat in ¼ cup crumbled blue cheese. Or combine butter and blue cheese in blender and blend at high speed.

Paprika Butter

ABOUT 1 CUP

For fish and broiled chicken.

Cream 1 cup butter and beat in 2 teaspoons paprika, 1 tablespoon lemon juice, 2 teaspoons wine vinegar and ½ teaspoon salt. Or combine all ingredients in blender and blend at high speed.

Maître d'Hôtel Butter

ABOUT 1¼ CUPS

For steak and broiled meats.

Cream 1 cup butter and beat in ¼ cup each minced parsley and chives and 3 tablespoons lemon juice. Or combine ingredients in blender and blend at high speed.

Blender Butter

Scandinavian, especially Danish, butter is infinitely superior to almost all butter sold in American markets. The reason for this is that the butter has, by law, a higher fat content and a lower water content than American butter, and that it is made much more carefully. The better quality of the Scandinavian butter also accounts for the unparalleled excellence of baked foods, which cannot be matched here at home. It is the reason why a Danish pastry in Denmark is a winged delight, whereas an American one plods on the ground.

In order to have butter that resembles the Scandinavian kind, one has to make it oneself, an easy enough task with a modern blender—in fact, it couldn't be easier. Blender butter is the sweetest butter imaginable and quite a revelation for those who never tasted it.

Sweet Butter

ABOUT 1 CUP

---

2 cups heavy cream   *½ cup iced water*

Pour cream into blender container. Cover and turn control to high speed. As soon as the cream is whipped, remove cover and pour in iced water. Blend a few seconds longer until butter forms. Pour into strainer and drain thoroughly. Knead with clean hands to extract any water that might be left in the butter.

Salt Butter

Add ¼ teaspoon salt to iced water and proceed as above.

Danish Blue Salad Dressing

ABOUT 1 CUP

Serve it on a salad of cold mixed vegetables, such as a combination of peas, carrots, cauliflower, celery knob cut in strips, boiled baby onions, and potatoes. Cook all vegetables separately before mixing for salad.

½ cup sour cream   *⅓ cup crumbled*
¼ cup mayonnaise   *Danish blue cheese*
1 tablespoon fresh
*   lemon juice*

Combine all ingredients and chill before using.

Norwegian Brown Onion Sauce

ABOUT 2½ CUPS

Good with meatballs, boiled meats, and cold leftover meat, and with boiled potatoes.

4 slices bacon, minced
1 medium-size onion, sliced
1 ½ tablespoons flour
2 cups bouillon, hot
½ cup cider vinegar

1 teaspoon salt
¼ teaspoon pepper
¼ teaspoon sugar
Dash of Kitchen
  Bouquet (optional)

Place bacon in cold saucepan and cook over medium heat until translucent. Add onion and cook until browned, but not burned. Stir in flour and cook until flour is browned, stirring constantly. Gradually stir in combined beef bouillon and vinegar. Season with salt, pepper, and sugar. If sauce is not sufficiently brown, add a dash of Kitchen Bouquet. Cook over medium heat 5 minutes, stirring constantly. Strain through fine sieve or purée in blender; the sauce should have the consistency of thick cream.

Scandinavian Caper Sauce

ABOUT 1⅓ CUPS

For pork chops and for fried fish and meats.

1 small onion, chopped
1 tablespoon butter
3 anchovy fillets, minced,
  or 2 teaspoons
  anchovy paste
3 tablespoons capers

3 tablespoons chopped
  parsley
1 ½ teaspoons flour
½ cup bouillon
½ cup mild vinegar

Brown onion in butter. Add anchovies, capers, and parsley. Stir in flour. Add bouillon and vinegar and simmer, covered, for 10 minutes, stirring frequently. (For a thinner sauce, add a little more bouillon.)

NOTE: If made for pork chops, pour sauce over chops before serving. If for fried fish or meats, serve separately.

Swedish Cold Sauce for Lobster and Seafood

ABOUT 1½ CUPS

---

1 cup mayonnaise
2 tablespoons heavy cream

1 tablespoon catsup
3 tablespoons Cognac

Combine all ingredients and blend thoroughly. Chill.

Scandinavian Cold Cucumber Sauce

ABOUT 1½ CUPS

For fish, shellfish, especially lobster, or meat.

1 large cucumber
¾ heavy cream
1 tablespoon white
   vinegar

½ teaspoon salt
¼ teaspoon white
   pepper

Peel, seed, and finely chop cucumber. Whip the cream until stiff and slowly add vinegar. Season with salt and pepper. Drain cucumber; fold gently into whipped cream.

Horseradish

Horseradish is especially popular in Denmark and Norway. Usually it is used fresh, since fresh horseradish is infinitely superior to the bottled or dehydrated variety. However, if you can't get the fresh horseradish, use the others. Try reconstituting dehydrated horseradish with lemon juice rather than vinegar.

Horseradish Cream for Fish and Shellfish

ABOUT 1¼ CUPS

Simple and excellent. Serve with boiled cod, haddock, shrimp, or lobster. Better not use it with trout or salmon, since the horseradish tends to overwhelm the unique delicate flavor of the fish.

1 cup heavy cream
¼ cup white vinegar
3 tablespoons finely
  grated horseradish

Salt and white pepper
  to taste
1 tablespoon finely
  chopped chives
  (optional)

Whip cream until stiff. Gradually add vinegar, stirring constantly. When cream has reached the consistency of thick mayonnaise, add horseradish, salt, and pepper. Sprinkle with chopped chives.

NOTE: A blander sauce, much to the taste of many Scandinavians, is made by omitting the vinegar.

Bottled Horseradish Cream

Combine 3 parts whipped cream with 1 part bottled horseradish. Season with salt and pepper to taste.

Horseradish Cream Sauce

ABOUT 1½ CUPS

Very popular in Scandinavia for nearly everything that is complemented by horseradish, such as boiled or fried meats and fish.

3 tablespoons butter
3 tablespoons flour
1 ½ cups light
   cream, hot

Horseradish to taste
⅓ cup heavy cream,
   whipped (optional)

Melt butter and add flour, stirring constantly until mixture is blended and smooth. Add hot cream all at once and cook until sauce is thickened and smooth, stirring all the time. Flavor with horseradish. Just before serving fold in whipped cream.

Sour Cream Horseradish Sauce

For smoked fish, cold seafood, or meats.

1 cup sour cream
Horseradish to taste
   (begin with 3
   tablespoons)

1 teaspoon sugar
⅛ teaspoon salt
1 to 2 tablespoons
   minced dill

Combine all ingredients except the dill. Chill, and just before serving add dill.

MAYONNAISE

Scandinavian cooking, especially Danish cooking, uses lots of mayonnaise. Buy the best kind you find, or make your own, which is a matter of minutes with an electric blender. Since every standard cookbook will give you a good mayonnaise recipe, I limit myself to the way of making it with a blender.

Blender Mayonnaise

ABOUT 1½ CUPS

Use a measuring cup with a lip; this will enable you to pour the olive oil in a thin, steady stream, which is important for success.

Juice of 1 large lemon   *1 egg*
½ teaspoon dry mustard   *1 cup olive oil*
½ teaspoon salt

Place lemon juice, mustard, salt, egg, and ¼ cup of the olive oil into the container of an electric blender. Cover; turn on the motor at low speed. Uncover immediately. Pour in remaining ¾ cup oil in a thin, steady stream. Scrape sides of blender with spatula. Mayonnaise will thicken almost immediately. If all the oil has not been incorporated into the thickened mayonnaise, flick on high speed and flick off at once. Repeat if necessary. Mayonnaise will keep 2 to 3 weeks under refrigeration.

Cognac Mayonnaise

ABOUT 1½ CUPS

For lobster or shrimp salads.
    Combine 1 cup mayonnaise with 1 small peeled, chopped and seeded tomato and 1 tablespoon Cognac.

Anchovy Mayonnaise

ABOUT 1 CUP

For fish or shellfish salads.
    Combine 1 cup mayonnaise with 1 tablespoon anchovy paste.

Rémoulade Mayonnaise

ABOUT 1½ CUPS

For fried fish, shellfish, fish, or cold meats.
    Combine 1 cup mayonnaise with ½ clove garlic, crushed, 2 teaspoons fresh or 1 teaspoon dried tarragon, 1 hard-cooked egg, finely chopped, ½ teaspoon prepared mustard, ½ teaspoon anchovy paste, and 1 tablespoon chopped parsley.

Scandinavian Curry Mayonnaise

ABOUT 1⅔ CUPS

For lobster, seafood, or chicken salads. A mild curry flavor is much appreciated by all the Scandinavians.

Combine 1 cup mayonnaise, 1½ to 2 teaspoons mild curry powder, 1 to 2 tablespoons lemon juice, 1 teaspoon sugar, and ½ cup heavy cream, whipped. Taste; if necessary, add more curry and lemon juice, very little at a time. (Scandinavians like their sauces blander than Americans.) Season with salt and pepper to taste. Chill. At serving time spoon over salad and toss gently.

Scandinavian Mushroom Sauce

ABOUT 1½ CUPS

For fish and other nonsweet soufflés; for fish and shellfish.

1 cup thinly sliced mushrooms	1 tablespoon Cognac
2 tablespoons butter	Salt and pepper to taste
1 cup heavy cream	

Cook mushrooms in hot butter until just tender. Add cream and Cognac and season to taste with salt and pepper. Heat through thoroughly, but do not boil.

Scandinavian Mustard Sauce

ABOUT 1 CUP

For *gravad lax* or other fish.

9 tablespoons olive or
    salad oil
3 tablespoons white
    vinegar
2 ½ tablespoons
    prepared mustard

¾ teaspoon salt
¼ teaspoon white
    pepper
¼ cup sugar
⅛ teaspoon ground
    cardamom

Combine ingredients and blend thoroughly. The sauce should be made at least 2 hours before serving. Beat with wire whip or fork before serving.

Danish Sharp Sauce

ABOUT 2 CUPS

For lobster, shrimp, or cold fish.

1 hard-cooked egg yolk
1 raw egg yolk
2 teaspoons prepared
    mustard (1 teaspoon
    if mustard is sharp)
2 teaspoons sugar

2 tablespoons white
    vinegar
Salt and pepper to
    taste
1 cup heavy cream,
    whipped

Sieve hard-cooked egg yolk. Mix it to a smooth paste with the raw egg yolk, the mustard, sugar, and vinegar. Season with salt and pepper to taste. Fold into whipped cream.

NOTE: If this sauce accompanies fish or shellfish cooked with dill, sprinkle 1 tablespoon minced dill on sauce before serving.

DESSERTS

*A*ll Scandinavians seem to be born with a sweet tooth, and it is a heartwarming sight to see a modern Viking as well as his foreign guests put away their second helping of a delicious, and preferably creamy, confection either as a dessert after a meal, with afternoon coffee, or as an evening snack. Traditional Scandinavian desserts are apt to be rich when made for company but more plain when they are for everyday family meals. Of a substantial nature, they cater to sweet teeth as well as to stomachs with a few remaining empty corners. As with all Scandinavian classic cookery, the more refined desserts are found in Denmark, made possible by a well-to-do country's proximity to Germany, a great dessert country.

Today's Scandinavians, especially the younger ones, no longer eat dessert as a matter of course; the reasons for this are basically the same as in the United States. As with baking, making desserts is not worth the time and effort unless it is done for a special occasion. So why skimp on butter, eggs, and cream when you make desserts at all, considering that the flavor of classic Scandinavian sweets depends on them? Make them authentically or don't make them at all, is what I think on the subject.

I am sorry that I was not able to give accurate yields or any yields at all for so many desserts, cakes, and cookies. The appeal of these goodies is largely a personal one, and it depends on many factors: how many courses are served before dessert; is the diner on a diet or too polite to disappoint the cook by refusing what he/she so lovingly prepared? It seems to me that the number of slices cut from a cake depends on who will eat it, when it will be eaten, and under what circumstances. Personally, I eat dessert only when I'm not full from the preceding courses. Sometimes I prefer a slice of fancy cake in the afternoon, with a cup of coffee. The size of cookies, too, depends on how they will be used. I remember my surprise at their different sizes in the various Scandinavian countries; yet the dough of these cookies turned out to be the same, or more or less the same, in each of these countries. I myself have made a few very large cookies or a large number of very small ones from the same amounts of dough given in the recipe.

Molded Cream Ring with Fruit

Fløderand med Henkogte Frugter

4 TO 6 SERVINGS

Very easy and very handsome.

3 eggs, separated
1/2 cup sugar
1 teaspoon vanilla
2 tablespoons unflavored
  gelatin

1/4 cup milk
2 cups heavy cream,
  whipped
Stewed fruit or frozen
  fruit, thawed

Beat egg yolks with sugar and vanilla until thick and lemon-colored. Dissolve gelatin in milk over hot water. Stir into egg mixture. Fold in whipped cream. Whip egg whites until they stand in peaks and fold into mixture. Rinse 1 1/2- or 2-quart ring mold with cold water. Sprinkle inside with sugar. Spoon in cream. Chill until set. Unmold and fill ring with any stewed fruit or thawed frozen fruit.

Mrs. Arne Christiansen's Fruit Salad

Frugt Salat

4 TO 5 SERVINGS

From a wonderful cook.

*2 cups mixed fresh fruit,
  such as apples, pears,
  grapes, bananas, oranges,
  apricots, peaches, and
  pitted sweet cherries
Lemon juice
2 eggs, beaten
3 tablespoons sugar*

*1 teaspoon vanilla
Juice of 1 lemon
Juice of 1 orange
½ cup heavy cream,
  whipped
Walnut halves
Red and green
  maraschino cherries*

Wash, dry, and prepare fruit, slicing thinly or dicing when necessary. If the peel is thin and crisp, the fruit does not need to be
peeled. Sprinkle fruit with a little lemon juice to prevent discoloring. Combine eggs, sugar, vanilla, and juice of lemon and
orange. Blend thoroughly. Cook in top of double boiler over
simmering, not boiling, water until mixture is thickened and
smooth. Do not let boil and stir constantly. Cool, stirring occasionally. When cool, fold in whipped cream and prepared fruits.
Chill. Decorate with walnut halves and red and green maraschino cherries.

Glacé Red Currants

Glacé Ribs

Very decorative for any dessert, but they must be eaten the day
they are made.

Wash red currant clusters but do not stem. Place on paper towels and blot dry. (If not thoroughly dried, the fruit will not take the glaze.) Whip whites of egg as stiffly as possible. Dip currant clusters into beaten egg white. Shake off surplus egg white carefully. Place on baking sheets lined with kitchen towels. Sprinkle with confectioners' sugar. Dry completely. Shake off surplus sugar before serving.

Frozen Cream

Frossen Fløde
ABOUT 4 SERVINGS

2 cups heavy cream, whipped
½ teaspoon vanilla

1 tablespoon sugar
Fresh fruit or canned fruit

Combine whipped cream with vanilla and sugar. Blend thoroughly. Spoon into refrigerator freezing tray and freeze until firm. Arrange mounds of fresh or canned fruits, peeled and sliced or diced (pineapple, peaches, raspberries, strawberries, apples, pears, etc.), on serving platter. Dip a serving spoon into hot water and spoon out frozen cream. Arrange around fruit and serve immediately.

Scandinavian Simple Vanilla Sauce

ABOUT 2 CUPS

For every kind of fruit pudding, for Swedish and Danish apple cake.

¼ cup sugar
1 tablespoon cornstarch
¼ teaspoon salt
2 egg yolks

2 cups light cream
 or milk
1 teaspoon vanilla

Combine sugar, cornstarch, and salt in top of double boiler. Add
egg yolks and blend thoroughly. Gradually stir in cream. Cook
over boiling water about 5 minutes or until mixture is thickened.
Stir constantly. Do not overcook. Remove from heat; cool and
add vanilla. Chill before serving.

Scandinavian Frosted Grapes

Used in elegant restaurants and homes to decorate platters of
cold ham, reindeer roasts, cold cuts.

Stem, wash, and dry perfect big blue grapes. First dip each
individual grape in slightly beaten white of egg; then roll in a
bowl of sugar. Or else, place sugar in paper bag and shake grapes
in it. Shake free of excessive sugar.

Scandinavian Fancy Vanilla Sauce

ABOUT 3½ CUPS

6 egg yolks, beaten
¼ cup sugar
2 cups heavy cream,
 heated

3 teaspoons vanilla
½ cup heavy cream,
 whipped

Combine egg yolks and sugar in top of double boiler. Beat until thick. Slowly add the heated cream, stirring constantly. Cook over hot, not boiling, water until thick, stirring all the time. Remove from heat; stir in vanilla. Cool, beating occasionally. At serving time, fold in whipped cream.

Wine Jelly

Portgelé

---

2 tablespoons unflavored
  gelatin
½ cup water
1 cup fresh orange juice
2 cups claret or port
  wine

1 tablespoon lemon
  juice
Sugar to taste
Whipped cream

Soften gelatin in cold water and dissolve over hot water. Combine orange juice, wine, and lemon juice. Add sugar to taste; if the wine is sweet, no sugar is needed. Stir in dissolved gelatin. Pour into glass serving dish and chill until set. Serve with whipped cream.

Danish Veiled Country Lass

Bondepige med Slør

Very good, but the dish must be made with pumpernickel or very dark rye bread.

4 cups finely grated, very
   dry pumpernickel or
   rye bread crumbs
3 tablespoons butter, in
   pieces
2 tablespoons sugar

2 cups thick applesauce
1½ cups heavy cream,
   whipped
2 tablespoons
   raspberry jam or
   currant jelly

Combine bread crumbs, butter, and sugar in heavy skillet. Sauté over medium heat, stirring constantly, until the bread crumbs are very crisp. Cool mixture. Place alternate layers of bread crumbs and applesauce in serving dish, ending with bread crumbs. Cover top with whipped cream. Decorate with raspberry jam or currant jelly. Chill before serving.

Variation
Substitute for 1 layer of applesauce a layer
of raspberry jam or currant jelly.

Variation
Add 1 to 2 tablespoons grated chocolate to
toasted bread crumbs. Use semisweet or
sweet baking chocolate.

Norwegian Eggedosis

Eggedosis is the national dish served in Norway on May 17, a date that corresponds to our Fourth of July. It is a thick egg cream, eaten from a dish with a spoon and served with cookies. The grownups cheer their *eggedosis* with a little brandy.

Eggedosis, which would make a simple dessert for American homes, is best made with an electric beater, since beating the eggs is the main trick. The basic proportions are 1 egg yolk beaten with 1 tablespoon of sugar. Some people add an egg white to a whole recipe of *eggedosis*, but it isn't really necessary.

Beat 8 egg yolks with 8 tablespoons sugar for 10 minutes with electric beater at medium speed. Spoon into glasses or small individual dishes and serve immediately. Children get their *eggedosis* plain, but for grownups pour a tablespoon of brandy into each glass before filling it with *eggedosis*.

Scandinavian Red Fruit Pudding

Rødgrød

ABOUT 4 SERVINGS

Perhaps the most famous of all Scandinavian desserts, and especially popular in Denmark. It is most delicious and refreshing and can be made with frozen berries as well. A mixture of berries is best, but you can also make *rødgrød* with one kind of berries only.

1 pint currants	⅓ cup cornstarch
1 pint raspberries	1 tablespoon lemon
2 cups water, or more	juice
1 cup sugar	⅓ cup blanched
¼ teaspoon salt	almonds (optional)

Trim and gently wash fruit. Drain; place in deep kettle with 1½ cups water. Simmer, covered, 10 minutes. Strain through fine sieve. Measure juice in kettle and, if necessary, add water to make 2½ cups liquid. Add sugar and salt. Heat to boiling point, stirring constantly. Mix cornstarch and ½ cup water; stir into fruit juice. Bring to a boil and cook 3 minutes, stirring constantly. Remove from heat; blend in lemon juice. Pour into glass serving dish and chill. Split blanched almonds into halves and decorate top of *rødgrød* in a star pattern. Serve with whipped cream.

Finnish Fruit Pudding

ABOUT 4 SERVINGS

A pudding widely eaten in all of Scandinavia.

One 11-ounce package mixed dried fruits
2 cups water, or more
1 cup light or dark corn syrup
¼ cup quick-cooking tapioca
¼ teaspoon ground cinnamon
¼ teaspoon grated nutmeg
⅛ teaspoon salt
Whipped cream

Combine fruit and water; simmer over low heat 30 minutes. Do not boil. Drain; reserve liquid and fruit. Add enough water to fruit liquid to make 1½ cups. Add syrup. Combine tapioca, cinnamon, nutmeg, and salt, and stir into fruit liquid. Let stand 5 minutes. Bring to a boil over medium heat, stirring occasionally. Remove from heat and let stand until slightly thickened. Pour half of the tapioca into a serving dish. Arrange fruit over tapioca. Cover with remaining tapioca. Cool. Garnish with whipped cream or serve with any vanilla sauce.

Rum Pudding

Rom-fromage

ABOUT 4 SERVINGS

---

6 egg yolks
1 cup sugar
2 tablespoons unflavored
   gelatin
⅔ cup cold water

½ cup blanched
   almonds, slivered
⅓ cup rum
2 cups heavy cream,
   whipped

Beat egg yolks until light. Beat in sugar, 2 tablespoons at a time, beating well after each addition. Soften gelatin in cold water and dissolve over hot water. Pour gelatin into egg mixture, stirring constantly. Stir in almond slivers and rum. Chill until mixture begins to thicken. Fold in whipped cream. Pour into rinsed 1½-quart mold and chill until set. Unmold and serve with raspberry sauce (recipe below) or any other fruit sauce.

RASPBERRY SAUCE

Hindbaer-sauce

ABOUT 1¾ CUPS

---

2 cups raspberries
⅓ cup sugar
1 tablespoon cornstarch

1 tablespoon water
1 tablespoon Cognac
   or rum

Combine raspberries with sugar and bring to boiling point, stirring frequently. Strain through a sieve or purée in blender. Add more sugar if necessary. Mix cornstarch and water to a smooth paste. Heat raspberry purée and stir in cornstarch. Cook, stirring constantly, until thickened and clear. Cool and stir in Cognac or rum.

Mrs. Johannes Laursen's Caramel Pudding

Karamelrand

4 TO 5 SERVINGS

---

1 ½ cups sugar
½ cup hot water
6 eggs, separated
2 cups heavy cream, heated

½ teaspoon vanilla
1 cup heavy cream,
   whipped
2 tablespoons brandy

Melt 1 ¼ cups sugar in heavy skillet. Stir until sugar is browned, but do not scorch. Pour two thirds of the caramel into the bottom of a warmed 1½-quart ring mold. Add ½ cup hot water to remaining syrup. Stir constantly over low heat until liquid and smooth. Set aside and cool. Beat egg yolks with remaining ¼ cup sugar. Gradually beat in heated cream and vanilla. Stir mixture until cooled. Beat egg whites until they stand in stiff peaks and fold into egg mixture. Pour into mold. Place mold in a baking pan with enough water to come up ⅓ the height of the mold, or about 1 inch. Bake in 350° oven 45 minutes to 1 hour, or until set. Chill. Combine whipped cream and brandy. Unmold pudding. Fold the cooled caramel sauce into the whipped cream. Serve on pudding or separately.

Delicate Norwegian Almond Pudding

3 TO 4 SERVINGS

1/4 cup cornstarch
1 cup milk
2 eggs, separated
1 cup heavy cream
1/2 cup sugar

1/4 cup finely ground
   almonds
1 tablespoon rum or
1 teaspoon rum
   flavoring

Mix cornstarch with 1/4 cup milk to a smooth paste. Beat in egg yolks. Combine remaining milk, heavy cream, sugar, and almonds in saucepan. Bring to a boil. Lower heat and stir in cornstarch mixture. Cook 5 minutes over low heat, stirring constantly. Remove from heat and stir in rum. Fold in egg whites, stiffly beaten. Pour into serving dish and chill. Serve with a warm fruit sauce.

Rhubarb Pudding

Rabarbergrød, Rabarbragrøt

3 TO 4 SERVINGS

Rhubarb, one of the first green things to grow after the long Scandinavian winter, is greeted with joy, especially in Denmark and Norway, and made into this favorite pudding.

2 pounds rhubarb,
   trimmed and cut in
   1/2-inch pieces
3 1/4 cups sugar
Water

3 tablespoons
   cornstarch
1 teaspoon vanilla
Heavy cream

Sprinkle rhubarb with sugar. Add water to cover. Bring to a boil, covered, and simmer until rhubarb is soft. Mix cornstarch with ¼ cup water to a smooth paste. Stir into rhubarb. Cook, stirring constantly, until thick and clear. Stir in vanilla. Pour into glass serving dish and sprinkle pudding with sugar. Chill and serve with heavy cream.

Mrs. Johannes Laursen's Orange Soufflé

Appelsin Fromage

3 TO 4 SERVINGS

Excellent. She has a great hand with desserts.

3 eggs, separated
½ cup sugar
2 tablespoons grated
   orange rind
¾ cup strained fresh
   orange juice
1 tablespoon
   unflavored gelatin

¼ cup cold water
2 cups heavy cream,
   whipped
Drained canned
   mandarin orange
   segments

Beat egg yolks until light. Beat in sugar, a tablespoon at a time, beating well after each addition. Stir in grated orange rind and orange juice. Soften gelatin in cold water and dissolve over hot water. Add to egg mixture, blending thoroughly. Chill until mixture begins to thicken. Fold in heavy cream and stiffly beaten egg whites. Spoon into glass serving dish and chill until set. Decorate top with drained canned mandarin orange segments and more whipped cream, if desired.

Lemon Delight

"Kan ikke lade vaere"

3 TO 4 SERVINGS

A refreshing dessert, good for a heavy meal. The Norwegian name means "I can't resist it."

5 eggs, separated
½ cup sugar
2 tablespoons unflavored
    gelatin

¼ cup cold water
Juice and grated rind
    of 2 lemons

Beat egg yolks with sugar until very thick and lemon-colored. Soften gelatin in cold water for 5 minutes. Heat over hot water, stirring until gelatin is dissolved. Add gelatin to lemon juice and lemon rind. Stir lemon mixture gradually into egg mixture. Blend thoroughly. Beat egg whites until they stand in peaks. Fold egg whites into lemon mixture. Pour into a rinsed 1-quart bowl or any serving dish. Chill until set. Serve covered with whipped cream or with a fruit sauce.

NOTE: This dessert improves upon standing for 1 day in the refrigerator.

Swedish Lemon Chiffon Cream

Citronkråm

3 TO 4 SERVINGS

Lemon creams turn up in all Scandinavian countries.

4 eggs, separated
½ cup sugar
Grated rind of 2 lemons
Juice of 2 to 3 lemons

½ cup dry white
wine
1 cup heavy cream,
whipped

In top of double boiler beat together egg yolks, sugar, and lemon rind until white and fluffy. Stir in lemon juice and wine, a little at a time, beating constantly. Place over hot, not boiling, water and beat with a wire whip or a rotary beater until mixture rises and thickens. Remove from heat and continue beating until cooled. Just before serving time fold in stiffly beaten egg whites and whipped cream. Serve with ladyfingers or macaroons.

NOTE: For festive occasions the lemon chiffon cream may be decorated with swirls of whipped cream topped with candied cherries.

Bittan's Orange Cream

ABOUT 4 SERVINGS

Bittan Valberg was a beautiful Swedish woman who designed and wove beautiful rugs, and cooked for fun.

12 small almond
   macaroons
¼ cup Curaçao liqueur
3 egg yolks
3 tablespoons sugar
1 cup light cream
Grated rind of 1 orange
Grated rind of 1 lemon
1 ½ tablespoons
   unflavored gelatin

¼ cup cold water
1 cup fresh orange
   juice
1 cup heavy cream,
   whipped
Whipped cream
Drained canned
   mandarin orange
   segments

Line bottom of glass serving dish with macaroons, and sprinkle with Curaçao. Combine egg yolks with sugar and beat until light and fluffy. Add light cream, a little at a time, and mix thoroughly. Stir in orange and lemon rinds. Cook over low heat until mixture thickens, stirring constantly. Be careful not to boil, or cream will curdle. Remove cream from heat. Dissolve gelatin in cold water. Add to warm cream and stir until thoroughly dissolved. Cool cream as quickly as possible by placing saucepan in bowl of iced water and stirring until cool. Add orange juice and fold in whipped cream. Pour mixture over macaroons. Chill until set. Decorate, with alternate swirls of whipped cream and drained mandarin orange segments.

Danish Prune Custard

Bagt Kraembudding med Svedsker

4 TO 5 SERVINGS

The Norwegians, too, are fond of this dessert.

> One 14-ounce package
> prunes, cooked
> Whole blanched almonds
> 3 eggs, separated
> 1/4 cup sugar

> 1 cup light cream
> 1 teaspoon vanilla
> 1 cup heavy cream,
> whipped

Set oven at 325°.

Pit prunes and replace pits with whole blanched almonds. Place in 1- or 1½-quart deep baking dish. Beat egg yolks with sugar. Bring light cream to a boil and stir into egg yolks. Add vanilla. Fold in stiffly beaten egg whites. Pour custard over prunes. Bake about 35 to 40 minutes, or until a knife inserted in the center comes out clean. Serve hot or cold with a topping of whipped cream.

Norwegian Prune Pudding

2 TO 3 SERVINGS

Another good dessert made with one of Norway's favorite fruits. It is inexpensive, easy to make, and children like it.

⅓ cup sugar
3 tablespoons cornstarch
¼ teaspoon ground cinnamon
½ cup prune juice

1 ½ cups pitted and chopped cooked prunes
1 tablespoon lemon juice

Blend sugar, cornstarch, and cinnamon in top of double boiler. Stir in prune juice and chopped prunes. Cook over boiling water until mixture thickens, stirring constantly. Cover and cook 10 minutes, stirring occasionally. Remove from heat, stir in lemon juice, and chill. Serve with any vanilla sauce or whipped cream.

NOTE: For a softer pudding, use ¾ cup prune juice.

Swedish Christmas Rice Porridge

Risgrynsgröt

3 TO 4 SERVINGS

Traditional dessert for Christmas Eve. The one who finds the almond will be married before the next Christmas comes around.

1 cup raw rice (do not use	½ cup heavy cream
converted rice)	1 whole blanched
1 cup water	almond
2 tablespoons butter	Ground cinnamon
4 cups milk	(optional)
½ teaspoon salt	Sugar

Wash rice under running water. Boil 1 cup water and add rice and 2 tablespoons butter. Cook, uncovered, over medium heat until water has disappeared. Stir frequently. Add milk and salt to rice. Simmer, covered, over lowest possible heat (or in top of double boiler over boiling water) until rice is tender and milk absorbed. Remove from heat and stir in heavy cream and almond. Place in serving dish and sprinkle with cinnamon and sugar. Serve with cold milk.

Finnish Rice-Apple Porridge

Riisi-omenapuuro

ABOUT 3 SERVINGS

---

6 medium-size tart apples	Grated rind and juice
⅔ cup raw rice, washed	of 1 large lemon
in cold water	¼ teaspoon salt
⅔ cup sugar	1 quart cold water

Peel, core, and thinly slice apples. Combine with all other ingredients in heavy saucepan. Simmer, covered, until rice is very soft and of a porridge consistency, stirring occasionally. Depending on the kind of rice used, this may take from 30 minutes to 1 hour. The finished porridge should be translucent and clear. Pour into dish and chill thoroughly. Serve with whipped cream and a fruit sauce, or with either alone.

Rømmegrøt, the Norwegian National Cream Porridge

3 TO 4 SERVINGS

The most famous of all the porridges that reach back into Norway's dark ages. It still is eaten in the countryside at weddings and other feasts. I think it is an excellent dish, provided the butter (see recipe below) is left out, and certainly worth making just to see what a centuries-old festive dish is like.

This cream porridge cannot be made with our commercial sour cream, which is processed to prevent the butter separation that is so essential to the original dish. If noncommercial sour cream is not available, make your own, as described in recipe.

2 cups heavy cream or
  2 cups noncommercial
  sour cream
2 tablespoons white
  vinegar or lemon juice

1 cup flour
2 cups milk, hot
Salt

Pour heavy cream into saucepan and stir in vinegar or lemon juice. Let stand 15 minutes. Bring cream mixture to a boil and boil gently for 5 minutes. Sprinkle with ½ cup of the flour and blend thoroughly. Continue cooking over low heat for 10 or more minutes, until butter comes to the surface. Beat constantly.

Skim off butter and keep hot. When no more butter oozes out of the porridge, sprinkle in remaining flour. Add hot milk, a tablespoon at a time, stirring all the time until porridge is thickened and smooth. Salt mildly to taste. Serve hot, with hot butter, black currant juice, cinnamon, and brown sugar.

CAKES

BAKING TIPS

Scandinavian women are great bakers, and there are literally hundreds of excellent recipes for breads, cakes, and cookies of all kinds. Many of these recipes resemble each other closely; the cookies, for instance, are almost always rich in butter and flavored with almonds. Then, too, most Scandinavian baking was produced with an eye for how long it would stay fresh, since in the old days the heating of the ovens was quite a production. Hence the hardtack breads, the rich cookies, that will remain fresh in airtight tins.

Many of the Scandinavian baking recipes crop up in all of the four countries. In the following chapter, I have chosen—and it was a most difficult choice—the ones that my friends and I, both here and in Scandinavia, found most suited to our American tastes.

Potato starch, or potato flour, is much used in Scandinavian baking. It gives the baked foods a long-lasting quality. Here, in the United States, potato starch is most easily found in Scandinavian neighborhoods and in Jewish food stores. Cornstarch can be substituted, without any change of proportions or baking method, for potato starch. Any recipe made with cornstarch in place of potato starch will have the same long-lasting quality. The recipes in this book have all been tested with cornstarch.

The old-time traditional Scandinavian raising agent, before baking powder became common, was hartshorn salt. This was made from the horns of the male deer that roamed the forests in profusion. Hartshorn salt makes cookies much crisper and lighter. The equivalent can be bought in any drugstore under the name of ammonium carbonate. Any reader eager for experimentation might try to add ⅛ to ¼ teaspoon of it to the baking powder in a recipe, provided he or she is not deterred by the strong ammonia odor. The resulting cookies will be crisper and lighter.

The flour used in the following recipes is all-purpose flour, sifted before measuring.

As for the almonds or nuts in the recipes, the instructions should be read literally. If a recipe, for instance, says: "⅓ cup sliced blanched almonds," the almonds were measured after slicing. But if the recipe says: "⅓ cup blanched almonds, sliced," the almonds were measured whole first, and then sliced. There is a difference in the volume of the almonds, depending on the way they are prepared.

Far too few cooks realize the importance of heating the oven properly. It takes any oven about 10 to 20 minutes to achieve the desired temperature. The correct temperature, right from the start of baking, is of the utmost importance to the success of the product. I cannot sufficiently recommend that my readers follow exactly the instructions given in the recipes as to when to light the oven.

Finally, some of the tortes in this book require a little practice. That means that a reader ought to try them out on the family before making them for company. And as the very last word, I suggest that the reader, before embarking on any baking project (or any cooking), read through the whole recipe and assemble all the ingredients before starting work.

Swedish Tosca Cake

Toscakaka

8 TO 12 SERVINGS

A good cake for a coffee party.

CAKE

2 eggs
1 cup sugar
1 teaspoon vanilla
1 cup sifted flour
1 ½ teaspoons baking
    powder

¼ teaspoon salt
¼ cup milk
½ cup butter or
    margarine, melted
Butter
Fine dry bread crumbs

TOPPING

¼ cup blanched almonds
¼ cup butter
3 tablespoons sugar

2 teaspoon heavy
    cream
1 tablespoon flour

Set oven at 325°.

Beat together eggs, sugar, and vanilla. Sift together flour, baking powder, and salt. Stir into egg mixture alternately with milk. Begin and end with flour. Beat in melted butter. Butter a 9-inch pie pan and sprinkle with bread crumbs. Pour batter into pan and bake 30 minutes or until cake tests done. While cake is baking, make topping.

Spread blanched almonds on baking sheet and warm in oven for 5 minutes. Slice warm almonds with a sharp knife. Combine almonds with all other topping ingredients and heat to boiling point, stirring constantly. Remove from heat and cool, stirring occasionally.

FINISHING TOSCA CAKE

After cake has baked 30 minutes and tests done, remove from oven. Turn up oven to 375°. Spread almond topping over top of cake. Place cake on cookie sheet and return to oven. Bake 10 minutes longer or until top is golden brown and bubbly. Serve warm, with whipped cream.

Danish, Norwegian Almond Ring Cake

Kransekake

12 TO 14 SERVINGS

This cake is really a tower of graduated almond paste rings, rising from the largest ring at the bottom to the smallest on top. It is popular in Denmark, and even more so in Norway, where it is served at Christmas, weddings, and other festive occasions. Since the almond paste can be bought, the cake is surprisingly easy to make and an excellent show piece. It is garnished with candy, cookies, and Norwegian or Danish flags.

CAKE

---

3 pounds almond paste,   4 to 5 egg whites,
  purchased or homemade   unbeaten
  (see page 194)   Confectioners' sugar

ICING

---

5 cups confectioners' sugar,   4 to 5 egg whites
  or more, sifted

Set oven at 300°.

To make cake: Heat almond paste over low heat until luke-warm, to make it pliable. With wooden spoon blend in egg whites. Knead with hands until firm and very smooth. (Knead hard; almond paste is not delicate.) Cover pastry board or any surface with confectioners' sugar. Coat palms of hands with confectioners' sugar, and keep them coated throughout shaping of almond paste rings. Roll dough with palms into 12 rolls ½ inch thick and in these length: 5, 6, 7, 8, 10, 12, 14, 16, 18, 20, 22, and 24 inches. Grease well and lightly flour brown paper the size of a cookie sheet. Place paper on cookie sheet. Place one roll at a time on paper and shape into a ring, pinching the ends together. Gently pinch each ring with thumb and forefinger with an upward movement so that rings will slope off into a sharp crease on top. Be careful to keep rings perfectly round. Bake about 20 minutes until light golden. Remove and cool on a smooth surface.

To make icing: Gradually stir confectioners' sugar into egg whites. Beat until mixture is smooth. Reserve one third. With decorating tube number 3 or 4, make loops of icing on each ring. Or drizzle icing over each ring with a spoon or a brush.

To assemble: Place largest ring on large serving plate or cake plate. Thinly spread top with reserved icing. Pile next largest ring on top, and repeat process. The icing helps the rings to stay on top of each other. End with smallest ring.

To serve, divide larger rings into sections and serve smaller ones whole.

Iceland Almond Cake Dessert

Mondlukaka

ABOUT 8 SERVINGS

Food in Iceland resembles very much the food of the other Scandinavian countries. This cake is good and easy, and it will keep well if wrapped in aluminum foil—without the filling and topping, of course.

1 cup butter	½ teaspoon baking
1 cup sugar	powder
4 eggs, separated	½ cup strawberry jam
1 teaspoon vanilla	1 cup heavy cream,
1 cup blanched almonds,	whipped and
ground fine	sweetened to taste
1 cup sifted flour	

Set oven at 350°.

Cream butter and gradually add sugar. Beat in egg yolks, one at a time, beating well after each addition. Stir in vanilla and almonds. Sift together flour and baking powder and gradually stir into batter. Beat egg whites until stiff but not dry, and fold into batter. Bake in three 8-inch buttered and floured layer pans about 30 minutes, or until golden brown. Cool 5 minutes before removing from pans. Spread strawberry jam between cooled layers and cover top and sides with swirls of whipped cream.

Swedish Cream Meringue Torte

ABOUT 8 SERVINGS

Meringue confections are one of the glories of Swedish baking. This torte can be put together with a cream filling, or with sweetened whipped cream and fruit, such as raspberries, strawberries, or blueberries.

CAKE

¾ cup butter
¾ cup sugar
6 eggs (yolks are used
    for cake, whites for
    meringue)
1 teaspoon vanilla
½ teaspoon almond
    extract

1 ¼ cups plus 1
    tablespoon sifted
    flour
1 ½ teaspoon baking
    powder
¼ teaspoon salt
½ cup milk

MERINGUE

6 egg whites
1 cup sugar
½ teaspoon vanilla

½ cup finely ground
    almonds or walnuts

ORANGE FILLING

⅓ cup flour
1 cup sugar
⅛ teaspoon salt
¼ cup water
1 ½ cups fresh orange
   juice

¼ cup fresh lemon
   juice
2 tablespoons grated
   orange rind
1 tablespoon grated
   lemon rind
4 egg yolks, beaten

TOPPING

2 cups heavy cream,
   chilled
2 tablespoons sugar

2 teaspoons vanilla
1 cup toasted almonds,
   cut in slivers

Set oven at 300°.

To make cake: With electric blender at low speed cream together butter and sugar for 3 minutes. Beat in egg yolks, one at a time, and then beat 3 minutes longer. Stir in vanilla and almond extracts. Sift together flour, baking powder, and salt. Add to batter alternately with milk. Grease and flour three 9-inch layer pans. Distribute batter in pans and smooth with knife or spatula.

To make meringue: Beat egg whites until stiff and dry. (Use an electric beater.) Gradually beat in sugar. Add vanilla and ground nuts. Continue beating until the meringue stands in stiff peaks. Spread meringue evenly on tops of the cake batter in the three pans. Bake 45 to 50 minutes or until cakes test dry. Cool on racks. Remove carefully from pans and brush free of crumbs.

To make filling: Combine flour, sugar, salt, and water and blend until smooth. Add orange and lemon juice and orange and lemon rinds. Cook until mixture thickens and is smooth and almost translucent, stirring constantly. Stir a small amount of the hot filling into the egg yolks. Return to saucepan and cook over low heat 3 minutes longer, stirring constantly. Remove from heat and beat until cool.

To make topping: In chilled bowl and with chilled beater whip cream until stiff. As cream begins to thicken, beat in sugar and vanilla.

To assemble the meringue torte: Just before serving, place one cake layer on cake plate, meringue side up. Cover with one third of the filling. Top with second layer, meringue side up. Repeat process, always placing layers meringue side up. Frost the top and sides of the torte with whipped cream topping and sprinkle with toasted almond slivers. Serve as soon as possible, and keep under refrigeration until serving time.

Fancy Lemon Filling for Meringue Cake

1 tablespoon cornstarch	*Grated rind and juice*
½ cup sugar	*of 2 small lemons*
½ cup water	*4 egg yolks, beaten*

Combine cornstarch and sugar. Blend with water to a smooth paste. Stir in lemon rind and juice. Blend in beaten egg yolks. Cook over lowest possible heat until filling is thick, stirring constantly. Beat until cooled.

Plain Filling for Meringue Cake

Use prepared pudding mix in any desired flavor, such as vanilla, lemon, chocolate, etc. Cook according to directions.

Apricot Filling for Meringue Cake

Combine ¾ cup thick apricot sauce, made from stewed, sweetened, and strained apricots (flavored with a little kirsch or brandy, if desired) and 1 cup heavy cream, whipped.

This is an excellent filling for any kind of layer cake.

Swedish Chocolate Dream Cake

Drömtårta

8 TO 10 SERVINGS

A jelly roll with a delicious filling. The filling is much creamier if made in an electric mixer.

CAKE

½ cup flour
⅓ cup cocoa, preferably
   Dutch type
1 ½ teaspoons baking
   powder
½ teaspoon salt
¼ teaspoon baking soda

3 eggs
3 tablespoons water
1 teaspoon vanilla
¾ cup granulated
   sugar
Confectioners' sugar

DREAM FILLING

¾ cup unsalted butter
1 egg yolk
¼ cup cocoa, preferably
    Dutch type

3 cups confectioners'
    sugar
3 tablespoons rum
    or Cognac

Set oven at 350°.

To make cake: Sift together flour, cocoa, baking powder, salt, and baking soda. Combine eggs, water, and vanilla and beat until thick and lemon-colored. Add granulated sugar gradually, a tablespoon at a time, beating thoroughly after each addition. Slowly sift flour mixture into egg mixture and fold in carefully, but thoroughly. Grease a 15- x 10-inch jelly-roll pan and line with waxed paper. Spread batter evenly in pan and bake 30 minutes or until cake tests done. Touch cake lightly with fingertip. If the dough springs back quickly, the cake is done. Sprinkle a kitchen towel heavily with confectioners' sugar. Turn cake onto towel and peel off waxed paper. Trim off crisp edges. Roll warm cake lengthwise in towel into a roll. Cool on rack, seam side down.

To make filling: Cream butter with egg yolk and cocoa. Beat in sugar gradually, alternating with rum. Keep at room temperature for spreading.

To assemble cake: Unroll cake and spread with filling. Re-roll and refrigerate until serving time.

Eat-Some-More Danish Tea Cake

6 TO 8 SERVINGS

From Mrs. Arne Christiansen, who lived in America but cooked in the best Danish manner. This cake is quick and easy to make.

½ cup butter or margarine
1 cup confectioners' sugar
2 eggs
Grated rind of 1 lemon
2 cups sifted flour
2 teaspoons baking
   powder

¼ cup milk
3 apples, peeled and
   thinly sliced
⅔ cup chopped
   blanched almonds
Granulated sugar to
   taste

Set oven at 350°.

Cream together butter and confectioners' sugar until mixture is fluffy. Beat in eggs, one at a time. Stir in lemon rind. Sift flour with baking powder. Add flour to batter, alternately with milk. Spread batter in buttered and floured 9-inch-square baking pan. Arrange apple slices on top of batter in overlapping rows. Sprinkle with almonds. Sprinkle with sugar; the amount depends on the sweetness of the apples. Bake 50 minutes or until cake tests done. Serve with sweetened whipped cream.

Swedish Cardamom Coffee Cake

ABOUT 10 SERVINGS

CAKE

1 ¼ cups milk
1 package dry yeast
¼ cup lukewarm water
¾ cup sugar
6 ¼ cups sifted flour

½ cup butter, at room
　temperature
¼ teaspoon salt
3 egg yolks
2 to 3 teaspoons
　ground cardamom

TOPPING

2 teaspoons ground
　cinnamon
2 tablespoons sugar

¼ cup chopped nuts
Milk

Scald milk and cool to lukewarm. Dissolve yeast in ¼ cup luke-warm water. Add to milk, with 1 tablespoon of the sugar. Beat in 3 cups of the flour. Cover and let rise until double in bulk, or about 1 to 1½ hours. Add butter, remaining sugar, salt, egg yolks, cardamom, and 3 cups flour. Reserve remaining ¼ cup flour for kneading. Turn dough onto floured surface and knead with floured hands until smooth and elastic. Place in greased bowl and turn to grease on all sides. Cover; let rise until double in bulk, or about 1 to 1½ hours. Divide risen dough in half, to make two cakes. Divide each half into 3 pieces and roll each piece into a strip 16 inches long. Pinch the 3 rolls together at one end, braid, and pinch ends together. Place cakes on ungreased cookie sheet. Let rise until double in bulk, or about 45 minutes.

Set oven at 375° 20 minutes before braids are ready to be baked. Make topping by combining cinnamon, sugar, and chopped nuts. Brush cakes with milk and sprinkle with topping.

Bake 25 to 30 minutes.

Danish Sand Cake

Sandkage

12 TO 14 SERVINGS

A very good and very popular, rather dry cake that keeps for a long time in an airtight tin. It has a fine, grainy quality that comes from including cornstarch in the ingredients. The cake does not need to be iced. For serving, sand cake should be cut into thin slices.

1 cup butter
1 cup granulated sugar
Grated rind of 1 lemon
6 eggs, separated
2 tablespoons brandy
1 cup sifted flour

1 cup sifted cornstarch
1 ½ teaspoons baking
   powder
½ teaspoon salt
Confectioners' sugar

Set oven at 350°.

Cream butter until fluffy. Gradually add granulated sugar, beating well after each addition. Stir in grated lemon rind. Beat in egg yolks, one at a time. Stir in brandy and beat again 3 minutes. Sift together flour, cornstarch, baking powder, and salt. Stir flour mixture into batter, beating thoroughly. Whip egg whites until stiff but not dry. Fold egg whites gently into batter. Grease thoroughly and flour a 9-inch tube pan. Pour batter into it evenly. Bake about 45 minutes or until cake tests done. Cool cake before removing from pan. Dust cake with confectioners' sugar before serving.

Norwegian Sponge Cake

Bløtekake

6 TO 8 SERVINGS

A favorite Norwegian cake, to be filled with whipped cream and jam, or with vanilla filling.

1 cup sifted confectioners' sugar
2/3 cup sifted cornstarch
3 eggs, separated
1/8 teaspoon cream of tartar
2 tablespoons water
1/2 teaspoon vanilla

1/2 cup strawberry jam
2/3 cup heavy cream, sweetened to taste and whipped
1 cup fresh or drained frozen whole strawberries

Set oven at 350°.

Sift 1/2 cup of the sugar and the cornstarch together 3 times. Beat egg whites, cream of tartar, and water in large bowl with rotary beater or electric mixer until mixture forms soft peaks. Beat in remaining 1/2 cup sugar a little at a time. Continue beating until stiff peaks form when beater is raised. Add egg yolks and vanilla; beat in just until well blended. Fold in sugar-cornstarch mixture a little at a time, and blend in thoroughly. Bake in two 8-inch greased and floured layer cake pans 30 minutes or until top springs back when touched lightly with finger. Let cool before removing from pans. Cut sides of cake away from the pans with a sharp knife. Spread strawberry jam on one cake layer. Cover with one third of the whipped cream. Top with second layer and spread remaining whipped cream over top and sides of cake. Garnish with strawberries.

Swedish Spice Cake

Kryddkaka

ABOUT 8 SERVINGS

CAKE

3/4 cup butter

1 1/2 cups firmly packed
brown sugar, sifted

3 eggs, separated

2 1/4 cups sifted flour

1 1/2 teaspoons baking
soda

1 1/2 teaspoons ground
cinnamon

3/4 teaspoon grated
nutmeg

3/4 teaspoon ground
cloves

1 cup buttermilk or
sour milk

1 cup heavy cream,
sweetened to taste
and whipped

CREAM FILLING

½ cup sugar	1 ½ cups milk or
1 ½ tablespoons	light cream
cornstarch	1 egg yolk, slightly
1 ½ tablespoons flour	beaten
⅛ teaspoon salt	¾ teaspoon vanilla

Set oven at 375°.

To make cake: Cream butter; add sugar, a little at a time, and beat until fluffy. Beat in egg yolks, one at a time. Sift together flour, baking soda, and spices. Add to egg mixture, alternately with buttermilk. Begin and end with flour. Beat egg whites until stiff but not dry and fold into batter. Pour into two 9-inch greased and floured layer cake pans. Bake about 20 to 25 minutes or until cake tests done. Cool and remove from pans.

To make cream filling: Sift together sugar, cornstarch, flour, and salt. Mix with milk or cream into a smooth paste. Cook over low heat until mixture thickens, stirring constantly. Cook all in all about 7 minutes. Stir some of the hot mixture into egg yolk. Return egg yolk mixture to sauce and cook 2 minutes longer, stirring constantly. Remove from heat and beat in vanilla. Cool before using (makes 1⅔ cups).

To assemble: Sandwich layers together with cream filling before serving and top with whipped cream.

Norwegian King Haakon's Cake

ABOUT 12 SERVINGS

King Haakon VII was the first king of Norway after the country declared her independence from Sweden in 1905. The cake can only be described as a rich, important one.

CAKE

1 cup butter
1 cup sugar
4 eggs, separated
1 teaspoon vanilla
1 cup sifted flour
1 cup sifted cornstarch

1 teaspoon baking
  powder
⅛ teaspoon salt
12 ounces almond paste,
  purchased or
  homemade

CHOCOLATE CREAM

3 tablespoons flour
1 cup light cream
⅛ teaspoon salt
½ cup sugar less 1
  tablespoon
4 egg yolks, beaten

1 teaspoon vanilla
5 tablespoons dark,
  unsweetened cocoa
  (Dutch type)
¼ cup heavy cream,
  whipped

ROYAL ICING

3 cups sifted confectioners'
   sugar
2 egg whites
¼ teaspoon salt

2 teaspoons lemon
   juice
1 teaspoon vanilla
Food coloring
   (optional)

DECORATIONS

Candied peel

Candied fruit
   (cherries, pineapple)

Set oven at 350°.

To make cake: Cream butter and sugar until thoroughly light and blended, about 3 minutes with an electric blender at low speed. Add egg yolks and vanilla and beat 3 minutes longer. Sift together flour, cornstarch, baking powder, and salt. Add to egg mixture, beating constantly for 3 more minutes. Beat egg whites until stiff but not dry and fold into batter. The dough should be soft and fluffy. Grease and flour three 9-inch layer pans. Divide dough into pans and smooth evenly with a knife or spatula. Bake about 25 to 30 minutes or until cake tests done and edges are slightly browned and shrink away from the pan. Cool cake in pans on cake rack for 5 minutes; invert on waxed paper.

To make chocolate cream: Mix flour with ¼ cup of the light cream to a smooth paste. Gradually add remaining cream, salt, and sugar, stirring constantly. Cook over medium heat until mixture thickens to the consistency of medium white sauce. Stir constantly. Stir a little bit of the sauce into the beaten egg yolks.

Add egg yolk mixture to balance of sauce. Cook over lowest possible heat 3 minutes longer, stirring all the time. Be careful not to boil, or cream will curdle. Remove cream from heat and stir in vanilla and cocoa. Cool as quickly as possible by placing saucepan in bowl of ice water and stirring until cool. Chill. Fold in whipped cream just before assembling cake.

ALMOND PASTE

This can be bought in Scandinavian specialty stores, or it can be made at home.

Combine 1 cup finely ground blanched almonds with ½ cup sugar, 1 small egg, ¼ teaspoon vanilla, and a few drops of yellow vegetable coloring. Mix thoroughly and knead with hands into a smooth paste.

To prepare almond paste: Between 2 sheets of waxed paper, with rolling pin, roll out almond paste to the size of a 9-inch layer pan. Trim edges, then set aside, in waxed paper.

To make royal icing: Combine all ingredients except food coloring in a bowl. With electric mixer at high speed beat until mixture is light and fluffy and stands in stiff peaks. If necessary, add a little more egg white or sugar to achieve correct spreading consistency. Add food coloring and beat in thoroughly. Do not underbeat; this icing can hardly, if at all, be overbeaten. Cover with a damp cloth when not in use; this method will keep the icing for several days at room temperature.

To assemble cake: Brush layers free of crumbs. Place one layer on cake plate. Spread with half of the chocolate cream and top with second layer. Spread with remaining chocolate cream and top with third layer. Peel the top piece of waxed paper from the circle of almond paste. Place almond paste on top layer of the cake and peel off the other piece of waxed paper, which is now on top. Frost cake with royal icing, beginning with the sides. Use knife or spatula dipped in cold water. The cake should be absolutely smooth.

To decorate: Cut candied peel into ⅛-inch strips. With these make the letter "H" and the Roman numeral "VII" in the middle of the cake. Cut a small crown from candied peel and place above initial. Around edge of cake place a decorative border of candied cherries, pineapple, and peel cut into fancy shapes. If you are a Norwegian, or wish to honor Norway, decorate further with small Norwegian flags.

Swedish Thousand Leaves Torte

Tusenbladstårta

10 TO 12 SERVINGS

A rich, handsome, and worthwhile Swedish specialty. It is important that the layers be very thin and crisp and that the applesauce used be of a tart and well-flavored variety. If the apples are too mild in flavor the torte will be too bland.

TORTE

2 cups sifted flour
1 cup cold butter

4 tablespoons iced water
6 tablespoons sugar

CUSTARD CREAM FILLING

1 ½ teaspoons unflavored
   gelatin
2 tablespoons cold water
2 egg yolks
3 tablespoons sugar

1 ½ tablespoons
   cornstarch
1 cup light cream
1 teaspoon vanilla
1 cup heavy cream,
   whipped

APPLESAUCE FILLING

1 ½ cups thick, tart, and well-flavored applesauce

LEMON ICING

2 tablespoons lemon
   juice

1 cup sifted
   confectioners' sugar

DECORATION

½ cup candied orange peel
½ cup blanched almonds
1 cup heavy cream

1 teaspoon sugar
½ teaspoon vanilla

To make torte layers: Sift flour into mixing bowl. With pastry cutter or two knives, cut in butter until pieces are the size of peas. While mixing with fork, add iced water gradually. Toss until dough just holds together. With hands, and handling as little as possible, shape into a ball. Chill for 30 minutes to 1 hour. Meanwhile, make custard cream filling.

To make filling: Sprinkle gelatin on cold water to soften. In top of double boiler combine egg yolks, sugar, cornstarch, and light cream. Cook over simmering, not boiling, water until smooth and thick, stirring constantly. Remove from heat and beat in gelatin and vanilla. Stir until gelatin is dissolved. Cool, beating occasionally. Fold in heavy cream. Chill. While filling is chilling, make icing.

To make lemon icing: Stir lemon juice gradually into confectioners' sugar, a little at a time, beating constantly, until spreading consistency has been achieved.

To bake layers: Set oven at 425°. Divide chilled dough into 6 portions. Use one portion at a time; keep others in refrigerator until used. Roll each portion between two sheets of waxed paper to a 9-inch circle. Use a 9-inch layer cake pan to measure circle, and trim off excess dough. Slide each layer onto a cookie sheet and peel off carefully the top sheet of waxed paper. (Or each portion may be rolled on bottom of 9-inch layer pan and trimmed.) Prick with fork all over, or layers will bunch during baking. Brush layers with iced water and sprinkle with 1 tablespoon sugar. Bake about 6 to 8 minutes or until golden brown. Cool on cookie sheets. Carefully peel off the bottom sheet of waxed paper. Sandwich layers together by spreading first layer with applesauce, second layer with custard cream filling, third layer with applesauce, fourth layer with custard cream filling and fifth layer with applesauce. Reserve top layer.

To decorate torte: Cut orange peel into strips. Ice top layer with lemon icing and place on top of other torte layers. Arrange orange peel strips in star pattern in the middle of the top layer. Toast almonds and chop coarsely. Sprinkle almonds around outer edge of cake. Whip cream with sugar and vanilla. With a pastry tube make rosettes of whipped cream on sides of torte, or frost sides with a spatula.

Swedish Mazarin Torte

Mazarintårta

ABOUT 10 SERVINGS

One of the most famous of Swedish cakes.

DOUGH

1⅓ cups sifted flour
1 teaspoon baking powder
⅓ cup sugar

½ cup butter
1 egg

FILLING

½ cup butter
⅔ cup sugar
1 cup ground blanched
   almonds

½ teaspoon vanilla
2 eggs
⅔ cup raspberry jam

LEMON ICING

1 cup sifted confectioners'
   sugar

1 tablespoon lemon juice
1 teaspoon water

To prepare dough: Into deep bowl sift together flour, baking powder, and sugar. Cut in butter and add egg. Mix together and knead with hands or spoon into a smooth dough. Chill while preparing filling.

To make filling: Cream butter; add sugar gradually and beat until fluffy. Add almonds and vanilla. Add eggs, one at a time, beating well after each addition.

To bake and assemble torte: Set oven at 350°. Roll out chilled dough between 2 sheets of waxed paper to fit bottom of 9-inch springform pan. Cut remaining dough into a strip and line sides of pan with it. Bring the dough at the bottom of the pan and the dough on the sides together so that they are tightly joined. (This is done to prevent filling from oozing out during baking.) Spread ⅓ cup of the raspberry jam over dough at bottom of the pan. Top with filling. Bake about 50 minutes or until torte tests done. Cool torte 10 minutes. Remove sides of pan and let torte cool entirely.

To make lemon icing: Combine confectioners' sugar, lemon juice, and water. Beat until smooth and of spreading consistency. When torte is cold, spread with remaining ⅓ cup jam. Dribble icing over jam.

Swedish Meringue Torte

6 TO 8 SERVINGS

A truly glorious creation. Meringues are easy to make if you have an electric beater and are willing to beat, beat, beat. They also must be baked in a slow, slow, slow oven. A proper meringue should be snow white for perfect taste, texture, and appearance. A slow baking accomplishes this.

6 egg whites	½ cup blanched
¼ teaspoon cream of tartar	almonds, ground
⅛ teaspoon salt	⅔ cup sifted
Grated rind of 1 lemon	cornstarch
1 ½ cups sugar	Filling of choice
	(recipes below)

Combine egg whites, cream of tartar, salt, and lemon rind in large bowl. With electric beater at medium speed beat until egg whites hold soft peaks. Beat in 1 cup sugar, one tablespoon at a time, beating constantly. Beat about 5 to 10 minutes longer, or until meringue is very thick and dull. Combine remaining sugar, almonds, and cornstarch. Sift into meringue and fold in quickly.

Set oven at 225°.

Grease and flour 2 large baking sheets. On plain, unwaxed brown paper, such as packing paper, trace and cut out four 8- or 9-inch circles. Spread a thin layer of meringue on each circle, using spatula. Smooth to end of paper and flatten top. Bake layers about 40 to 45 minutes, or until they are crisp and dry, but still white. Cool; remove layers carefully from paper.

You can fill a meringue tart with anything that takes your fancy. Creamy fillings and fruit fillings, plus whipped cream, and ice cream, combine well with the crispness of the tart. Here are two fillings the Swedes and other Scandinavians like.

STRAWBERRY FILLING

2 cups sliced sweetened	2 tablespoons kirsch,
strawberries, drained	Cognac or Cointreau
3 cups heavy cream,	(optional)
whipped	½ cup blanched
	almonds, halved

Fold together strawberries and 2 cups of the whipped cream. Blend in liqueur. Spread on three of the meringue layers. Cover top layer with remaining whipped cream, preferably in an ornate design of swirls and rosettes. Use a pastry bag with a star tip. Stud whipped cream top with almonds. Chill tart before serving.

CHOCOLATE FILLING

One 6-ounce package dark sweet chocolate pudding, made with half milk, half cream

1 cup heavy cream, whipped
1 cup toasted almonds, halved

Cook chocolate pudding according to package directions. Chill; fold in ½ cup whipped cream. Spread pudding between meringue layers; leave top layer plain. Cover top layer and sides of cake with remaining whipped cream, tracing decorative swirls. Stud top and side of cake with toasted almond halves. Chill before serving.

NOTE: A meringue tart with chocolate filling is sometimes called a *rolla tårta.*

Rødvig Kro Apple Tart

Aebletaerte med Crème Fraîche

8 TO 10 SERVINGS

TART PASTRY

½ cup butter
½ cup sugar
2 egg yolks

½ teaspoon almond extract
1 ¼ cups sifted flour

FILLING

1 ½ cups light cream
2-inch piece of vanilla
    bean
½ cup sugar
¼ cup flour
4 egg yolks, well beaten
½ cup heavy cream,
    whipped

3 large well-flavored
    apples, on the tart
    side
Salted water
⅔ cup sugar or more,
    depending on
    tartness of apples
1 ½ cups heavy
    cream, whipped

Set oven at 350°.

To make pastry: Cream butter with sugar until fluffy. Beat in egg yolks, one at a time, beating well after each addition. Stir in almond extract. Beat in flour. Pat dough into bottom and sides of 9- or 10-inch round springform pan or deep pie pan. Use preferably a pan with a detachable bottom since the tart cannot be unmolded. Bake about 30 minutes. Cool.

To make filling: Scald light cream with vanilla bean. In top of double boiler, beat together sugar, flour, and egg yolks until smooth. Place over (not into) simmering water. Remove vanilla bean from scalded cream and add cream gradually to egg mixture, stirring constantly. Cook, stirring constantly, until mixture just reaches the boiling point. Remove from heat and cool, stirring frequently. Fold whipped cream into cold custard.

To assemble tart: Spoon cold custard into cooled tart pastry. Peel and core apples, and cut into thin slices. Drop slices into salted water to prevent discoloration. Drain and dry apple slices and pile on custard in the shape of a dome. Preheat oven to 450°. Sprinkle sugar over apples. Place in oven just long enough to melt sugar. Pipe whipped cream over apples in decorative designs.

A FAMOUS CHEF'S RECIPES

The pastry bun we know as a "Danish" is called *wienerbrød* in Scandinavia, which translates into "Viennese bread," and it is made with a puff-pastry type of dough. There are any number of recipes for *wienerbrød*, and thus I have chosen my favorite one, because it stands as a prototype for all *wienerbrød*. It was given to me, along with other recipes that follow, by Chef G. L. Wennberg, a tall, kindly man of Swedish origin who was one of the most famous chefs in all of Scandinavia. At the time I met him years ago, he was pastry chef at the Hotel Angleterre in Copenhagen. I remember that once, when I came to this lovely hotel from North Lapland in early January, Chef Wennberg's famous *wienerbrød* was waiting for me, with a pot of hot chocolate, in the lobby of the hotel, which was filled with masses and masses of blooming white lilac. To this day I think of the scene as totally, absolutely wonderful.

Chef Wennberg was a master pâtissier in the great French tradition of Carême and other famed pastry chefs of the eighteenth and nineteenth centuries. His cakes tasted as wonderful as they were to look at. With his approval, I adapted them for the American home cook to keep their appearance and flavor as close to the originals as possible.

First, a few tricks for making *wienerbrød*. Personally, I have found it easier to make the Danish with unsalted margarine, as so many Danes make theirs. Margarine can be easier to handle because it is generally more malleable than the various kinds of American butter, which can vary from region to region and from season to season. Remember also to keep your pastry cool; Chef Wennberg once told me that he could not make his own flaky *wienerbrød* on a hot day (or what a Scandinavian but not an American would call a hot day). He added that all Danish pastry should be eaten as soon as possible after baking. I discovered, however, that *wienerbrød* will freeze quite well if cooled and wrapped properly and tightly in foil or freezer wrap. Do not keep it in your freezer more than 3 months, and thaw before serving. Or reheat the thawed pastries slightly in a preheated moderate (375°) oven for about 2 to 3 minutes.

If any of my readers should not turn out to be a perfect baker of Danish pastries, he or she should take heart. In Denmark, these *wienerbrød* are almost invariably bought at a bakery that specializes in them.

Before embarking on the recipe, I suggest reading the following observations made by Chef G. L. Wennberg. I've tried to keep them as much as possible in his own language.

"It is important to make sure that the dough and the butter are the same temperature and of the same consistency. If the butter is too hard in comparison with the dough the resulting pastry will be uneven and lumpy. The butter should not be too soft as it then breaks through the dough on being rolled, thus spoiling the layers.

"A really delicious and attractive piece of Danish pastry is a true delight and can be achieved only by the confectioner or baker who has sufficient interest and fondness for his trade. It is also important to take care over forming the pastry, to allow it to rise properly and to see to it that it is baked right away. Danish pastry should never be allowed to rise in a very moist atmosphere, or in too dry heat, but should be left to rise slowly in a warm, slightly moist place. If the dough is left to rise in an overheated room, the butter will melt out of the dough and if left to rise in too dry a heat the dough will form a crust. The length of time that the dough should be left to rise varies in accordance with the kind of Danish pastry to be produced. Danish pastry should always be put into a very hot oven and then baked slowly at a more moderate temperature. Danish pastry tastes best fresh from the oven."

Danish Pastry Basic Recipe

Wienerbrød à la Wennberg

---

2 packages dry yeast
¼ cup lukewarm water
¾ cup milk
2 tablespoons sugar
1 whole egg
1 egg yolk
¼ teaspoon salt
1 teaspoon ground
  cardamom

1 pound unsalted
  butter or unsalted
  margarine (use 6
  tablespoons to
  prepare the dough)
4 ⅓ cups sifted
  all-purpose flour

Dissolve yeast in lukewarm water. Stir until completely dissolved. Heat milk to lukewarm. Beat in sugar, egg, egg yolk, salt, cardamom, and 6 tablespoons of the margarine or butter. Stir in dissolved yeast. Beat in flour. Turn dough out on a floured board and knead until smooth, soft, and pliable. Cover dough and allow it to rise until doubled in bulk. Punch down and roll dough into a 12-inch square. Work remaining margarine or butter under iced water until soft and pliable. Knead until all the water has oozed out. Shape the butter into a square and place it on the dough. Working quickly, pat the butter with the finger tips so that the entire surface of the dough is covered with butter. Cover dough with sheet of waxed paper. With a cold rolling pin (chill it in the refrigerator) roll out dough into an oblong shape. The dough should be about ½-inch thick or thinner. Remove waxed paper. Fold the sheet of dough into thirds. Chill in the refrigerator for 10 minutes. Repeat the rolling, folding, and chilling process twice more. Roll out again to a ½-inch-thick oblong, but fold in half. Chill in the refrigerator for 30 minutes. (Dough should be rolled, folded, and chilled 4 times altogether.) Line cookie sheets with foil and turn up edges. (This is to prevent butter from oozing into oven during baking.) Shape pastries and place at least 3 inches apart on foil-lined cookie sheets.

Preheat oven to 400° and lower temperature to 350° when pastries are placed in oven.

Cream Buns

Cremeboller

---

1 recipe Danish pastry
(see above)

Very thick vanilla
pudding
Beaten egg yolk

Roll out chilled dough to ⅓-inch thickness. Cut dough into 4-inch squares. Place a spoonful (the size of a walnut) of thick vanilla pudding in the center of each square. Fold the four corners around the pudding. Place on foil-lined cookie sheet with folds facing downward. Press lightly on top and brush with beaten egg yolk. Allow to rise for 15 minutes. While pastries are rising, preheat oven to 400°. Lower temperature to 350° when placing pastries in the oven. Bake for 15 to 20 minutes, or until golden brown.

Spandauers

Spandauer

---

1 recipe Danish pastry   Raspberry jam
   (see page 205)   Beaten egg yolk

Proceed as for cream buns (above), but use raspberry jam for filling instead of vanilla pudding.

Carnival Buns

Fastelavnsboller

---

1 recipe Danish pastry   Beaten egg yolk
   (see page 205)   Thin water icing
Raisins   (see page 209)
Chopped mixed candied
   peel

Roll out chilled dough to ⅓-inch thickness. Cut dough into 4-inch squares. Place a few raisins and a little chopped candied peel in the center of each square. Fold the 4 corners around fruit. Proceed as for cream buns (see page 206), but ice the carnival buns with a little thin water icing while still warm.

Triangles

Trekanter

---

1 recipe Danish pastry
(see page 205)
Pastry filling
(recipe below)
Beaten egg yolk

Chopped walnuts or
almonds
Thin water icing
(see page 209)

Roll out chilled dough to ⅓-inch thickness. Cut into 4-inch squares. Place 1 heaped teaspoon pastry filling in the center of each square. Fold over to form a triangle. Press edges together, sealing in filling. Slash edges with a sharp knife 5 or 6 times. Place on foil-lined cookie sheets. Brush pastries with beaten egg yolk and sprinkle with chopped nuts. Allow to rise for 15 minutes.

While pastries are rising, preheat oven to 400°. Lower temperature to 350° when placing pastries in the oven. Bake for 15 to 20 minutes, or until golden brown. Top with a little thin water icing while still warm.

PASTRY FILLING

Remonce

½ cup butter
½ cup sugar

1 ½ teaspoons vanilla

Cream butter and sugar until light and fluffy. Stir in vanilla. Use for Danish pastries.

THIN WATER ICING

About 1 ½ cups
confectioners' sugar

About 1 ½ to 2
tablespoons water,
lemon or orange
juice, or any other
liquid flavoring

Sift confectioners' sugar into a bowl. Gradually stir in the water or other liquid flavoring, 1 teaspoon at a time, beating vigorously to make a smooth paste. You may have to add a little more sugar to make the desired consistency, since both the liquid and the confectioners' sugar may vary, but only a very little, about ½ teaspoon at a time.

NOTE: You may also use rum for flavoring.

Scrubbing Brushes and Combs

Skrubber og Kamme

ABOUT 12 PASTRIES

The first steps for making these two differently shaped Danish pastries are similar.

1 recipe Danish pastry
(see page 205)
Pastry filling
(see page 208)

Beaten egg yolk
Sugar
Finely chopped
walnuts or almonds

Roll chilled dough into a rectangle measuring 20×6 inches. Cut the dough lengthwise into two strips. Spread a pencil-thick strip of pastry filling down the center of the two strips of dough. Fold one third of the dough lengthwise over the filling. Brush dough with beaten egg yolk. Fold other side over the first. You should now have a long three-layered strip of dough. Press down lightly. Turn upside down and brush smooth side with beaten egg yolk. Combine sugar and nuts.

To shape scrubbing brushes: Cut strip of dough into 12 pieces, making diagonal cuts. Dip pieces in sugar-nut mixture and place on foil-lined cookie sheets. Allow to rise 15 minutes. While pastries are rising, preheat oven to 400°. Lower temperature to 350° when placing pastries in the oven. Bake for 15 to 20 minutes, or until golden brown.

To shape combs: Cut strip of dough into 12 pieces, making straight cuts. With a sharp knife, gash one side of each piece 4 or 5 times, cutting evenly toward the filling, but without touching the filling. Dip pieces in sugar-nut mixture and proceed as above.

Chef Wennberg's Orange Meringues

ABOUT 12 MERINGUES

In spite of the long recipe, this spectacular dessert is not difficult to make. The meringue shells and the filling can be prepared in advance, but they must be assembled and glazed just before serving.

MERINGUES

---

5 egg whites, at room
    temperature
1 ⅔ cups granulated sugar

2 teaspoons grated
    orange rind
Sifted confectioners'
    sugar

ORANGE MOUSSE

¾ cup sugar
½ cup fresh orange juice
4 egg yolks

2 teaspoons grated
   orange rind
2 cups heavy cream

FONDANT ICING

---

1 ½ cups granulated sugar
¾ cup water
1 ½ tablespoons light corn
   syrup
6 ½ cups sifted
   confectioners' sugar

1 tablespoon grated
   orange rind
Yellow food coloring
2 ounces sweet
   chocolate, melted

To make meringues: Beat egg whites until stiff. Beat in granulated sugar, 1 tablespoon at a time, until mixture is very stiff. Fold in grated orange rind. Line cookie sheets with unglazed brown paper. With a spoon or a pastry bag, shape meringue into mounds resembling half an orange. Sprinkle meringues with confectioners' sugar. Bake in 275° oven about 40 minutes, or until meringues are crusty. Remove meringues from brown paper. Turn upside down and hollow out carefully with a teaspoon. Take care not to break shell. Store in airtight container until ready to use.

To prepare orange mousse: Over medium heat, boil granulated sugar and orange juice for 5 minutes. Beat egg yolks in top of double boiler until very thick. Gradually beat in orange syrup. Beat over hot, not boiling, water until smooth and thick. Fold in grated orange rind. Remove from hot water and beat until cool. Whip cream and fold into cooled orange custard. Pour mixture into a freezing tray and freeze until firm. Stir several times during freezing process to prevent iciness.

To prepare fondant icing: Combine granulated sugar, water, and corn syrup. Bring mixture to a boil and cook until clear. Remove from heat and cool for 5 minutes. Gradually beat in confectioners' sugar and grated orange rind. Beat until smooth and lukewarm. Keep over hot, not boiling, water. Color with yellow food coloring until a bright orange.

To assemble orange meringues: Fill meringue shells with orange mousse and press 2 shells together to form one orange. Place filled meringues on wire rack over waxed paper and spoon entire surface with fondant icing. Let icing harden. With a thin brush, dot the top of the orange meringue with a little melted chocolate to resemble the stem of an orange. Serve immediately.

NOTE: Leftover icing can be cooled and reheated for other use. It may then be necessary to add a few drops of water to icing in order to thin it for spreading consistency.

Chef Wennberg's Superlative Chocolate Orange Cake

10 TO 12 SERVINGS

This cake is different from our chocolate cakes; it is drier and fragrant with orange. The keeping qualities are excellent. It is also easy to make.

CAKE

2 3/4 cups flour
3/4 cup Dutch-type cocoa
3 teaspoons baking powder
Grated rind of 4 large
   oranges
2 cups (1 pound)
   unsalted butter

1 3/4 cups sugar
4 eggs
3/4 cup lukewarm
   water
3/4 cup milk

CHOCOLATE COATING

Three 4-ounce bars sweet baking chocolate

MARZIPAN COATING

2 cups almond paste,
   purchased or homemade
   (see page 194)

Green food coloring

DECORATION

Candied violets, roses, and mimosa

Set oven at 350°.

   To make cake: Sift flour with cocoa and baking powder. Stir in orange rind. Cream butter until soft. Gradually beat in sugar,

2 tablespoons at a time, beating well after each addition. Beat in eggs, one at a time, beating well. Combine water and milk. Alternately add flour mixture and milk to the batter, beginning and ending with flour. Pour into greased and floured 13- ×4-inch baking pan. Bake in oven about 1 hour, or until cake tests done. Let stand at room temperature for about 5 minutes before unmolding.

To make chocolate coating: Melt chocolate in the top of a double boiler. Stir until very smooth. Spread with a pastry brush over cooled cake. Smooth with a warmed spatula or knife. Coating must be very smooth. Chill until firm.

To make marzipan coating: If almond paste is too stiff to handle, warm slightly in top of double boiler. Work in sufficient green food coloring for desired shade. Between 2 sheets of waxed paper, roll out almond paste to ¼-inch thickness or thinner. Roll it long and wide enough to cover the top and sides of the cake. Remove 1 sheet of waxed paper. Flip almond paste onto cake and remove the second sheet of wax paper. Trim edges of marzipan to fit around cake. Cake must be completely covered with almond paste. Use remaining almond paste to decorate cake with hearts, bows, or any desired shapes. Finally, decorate cake with candied violets, roses, and mimosa. (These can be bought imported from France in specialty stores.)

King Frederik's 50th Birthday Cake

12 TO 14 SERVINGS

Chef Wennberg made this cake for King Frederik IX, the past king of Denmark. The original cake was exquisitely decorated with a picture of Amalienborg, the royal residence, executed in cocoa, and decorative crowns, initials, and dates were piped onto the cake with gilt icing.

The cake is in the shape of an ancient book, and according to American standards, it is not a cake proper but a confection of almond paste and fillings. Only a skilled confectioner could reproduce the magnificent decorations, and I have therefore omitted the picture of Amalienborg and other details from the recipe that follows. However, a very creditable replica of the original will be achieved—a truly magnificent confection.

I must warn my readers that this is *not* a cake for beginners. The almond paste can be homemade or bought imported from Denmark in specialty stores.

CAKE LAYERS

6 cups almond paste,
   purchased or homemade
   (see page 194)

About ½ cup Cognac
½ cup Peter Heering
   cordial

VANILLA CUSTARD FILLING

2 cups light cream
¼ cup butter
⅔ cup flour
⅔ cup sugar
½ teaspoon salt

1 cup light cream, cold
4 egg yolks, well
   beaten
2 teaspoons vanilla

BUTTERCREAM FROSTING

1/2 cup butter
About 1 pound sifted
    confectioners' sugar

2 egg yolks
1 1/2 tablespoons
    Cognac

BOOK COVER

4 1/2 cups almond paste
Cocoa

Yellow food coloring

DECORATORS' ICING

2 1/2 cups sifted
    confectioners' sugar

1/4 cup egg whites
Yellow food coloring

Set oven at 300°.

To make cake layers: Divide almond paste into four pieces. Roll out each piece between two sheets of waxed paper to 1/8-inch thickness and into a sheet measuring 8×10 inches. There should be four 8- ×10-inch sheets. Line cookie sheets with unglazed brown paper. Lightly grease brown paper. Remove top piece of waxed paper from almond paste sheets. Flip sheet of almond paste, uncovered side down, onto cookie sheet. Peel off remaining piece of waxed paper. Repeat until all four sheets of almond paste are on cookie sheets. Bake for 15 to 20 minutes or until deep brown, puffed, and dry to the touch. Remove from oven. Cool to lukewarm. Flip sheets of almond paste carefully onto a rack. Remove brown paper carefully. Cool layers. Sprinkle 2 layers with Cognac and 2 with Peter Heering.

To make vanilla custard filling: Combine 2 cups cream and butter and heat until butter is melted. Combine flour, sugar, salt, and 1 cup cold cream. Stir until smooth. Gradually stir into hot cream. Cook over low heat, stirring constantly, until smooth and thick. Beat egg yolks. Add some of the hot mixture to egg yolks. Blend well. Add egg mixture to the hot mixture. Cook, stirring constantly, for another 5 minutes. Cool slightly and stir in vanilla. Do not chill. Place one sheet of baked almond paste on a large serving platter. Cover with one third of the warm vanilla custard. Repeat, using all four layers of almond paste, ending with almond paste. Cool. Trim cake to make all four edges even.

To make buttercream frosting: Cream butter until fluffy. Gradually beat in half of the confectioners' sugar. Beat in egg yolks. Gradually beat in Cognac. Beat in remaining sugar gradually until frosting can be spread easily.

To prepare book cover: Take 2¼ cups of the almond paste and work cocoa into it to make a medium mahogany-brown color. Take ⅔ cup of the remaining white almond paste and tint it with yellow food coloring to a golden color. Take remaining white almond paste and roll it to ¼-inch thickness. Cut it into long strips to fit and cover one 10-inch and two 8-inch sides of the cake. Before placing the strips on the side of the cake, mark the strips in grooves lengthwise with the back of a knife to resemble the pages of a book. Take 1 cup of the brown almond paste and roll it to ¼-inch thickness. Cut it into a strip to fit and cover the other 10-inch side of the cake. This represents the spine of the book and should be marked accordingly. Take ½ cup of the brown almond paste and again roll it to ¼-inch thickness. Cut into a 4- ×6-inch oblong and into two triangles of the same size. Reserve. The oblong will bear the inscription of the cake and the triangles will represent the corners of the book. Take the remaining brown, yellow, and white almond paste and knead it together until a marbled color is achieved. Roll out to ¼-inch thickness. Trim to the same length and width as the cake. This is the cover of the book. Place it accordingly on the top of the cake. Now place the brown oblong at the center of the top of the cake, on the marbled cover. Place the triangles on the upper and lower corners of the cake. The "book" is now made and ready for decorating with decorators' icing.

To make decorators' icing: Combine confectioners' sugar and egg whites and beat with an electric beater until icing holds its shape. Tint with yellow food coloring to a golden color. Decorate the oblong in the center, using the writing tip of a pastry tube, with a crown and initials of H. M. King Frederik IX and H. M. Queen Ingrid of Denmark, as was the original cake. Decorate spine accordingly.

NOTE: Of course, the cake may be decorated with any other designs or initials.

Princess Margrethe's Almond Garland

ABOUT 10 TO 12 SERVINGS

Chef Wennberg created this elegant dessert cake in honor of the then Danish heir to the throne who is now Denmark's queen. The blanched almonds must be ground extremely fine, and I advise the use of an electric blender or food processor. Next best to these is a nut grinder—the nuts must be ground 4 times. On no account use a meat grinder, because nuts ground in a meat grinder are apt to be oily.

CAKE

------

2 ½ cups finely ground blanched almonds	Spun sugar (optional)
10 egg whites	Fresh strawberries, unhulled
¾ cup sugar	Curaçao
3 tablespoons Peter Heering cordial	Sugar
	Blanched almonds

CHOCOLATE GLAZE

------

1 ½ squares unsweetened chocolate	1 ½ cups sifted confectioners' sugar
3 tablespoons unsalted butter, melted	½ cup chopped walnuts
3 tablespoons rum	½ cup chopped pistachio nuts

Set oven at 350°.

To make cake: Combine ground almonds with 2 egg whites and sugar in a small saucepan. Heat mixture to lukewarm over low heat, stirring constantly. Remove from heat and stir in Peter Heering. Cool. Beat remaining 8 egg whites until they stand in stiff peaks. Fold egg whites into almond mixture. Grease a 9-inch ring mold. Pour mixture into ring mold. Place in a pan of water, allowing the water to reach halfway up the mold. Bake in 350° oven for 30 to 35 minutes. Remove ring mold from water and cool on rack for 10 minutes. Unmold carefully on large serving platter, preferably silver, to cool completely.

To make glaze: In top of a double boiler, melt chocolate

over hot water. Add butter and stir until butter is melted. Add rum and confectioners' sugar. Beat mixture until smooth. While warm spread quickly over the cooled almond garland.

Sprinkle chopped walnuts and pistachios over chocolate glaze. Fill the center of the ring with fruit salad. Top the ring with a crown made of spun sugar. (For spun sugar recipe, consult standard or candy cookbook.) Sprinkle unhulled strawberries with Curaçao and dip in sugar. Place strawberries around the ring alternately with blanched almonds. Serve with half-frozen custard sauce.

FRUIT SALAD

The idea is to have a colorful combination of fruits. About 2 to 3 cups of fruit salad are needed. Combine orange sections (free of white membrane), apricots, peaches, strawberries, or any other suitable fruit. Sprinkle fruit with a little lemon juice to prevent discoloring and flavor with Curaçao. Chill for 1 hour. Drain fruit before filling center of the ring with it.

HALF-FROZEN CUSTARD SAUCE

Freeze vanilla custard filling (page 215) until mushy. Beat twice during freezing process to avoid graininess.

PASTRIES
AND
COOKIES

Swedish Saffron Buns or Lucia Buns

ABOUT 18 BUNS

These buns are traditionally served on St. Lucia's Day, December 13, the beginning of the Christmas season. On that day a young daughter of the house puts on the traditional white robe and crown of evergreens and lighted candles, and goes from bedroom to bedroom serving saffron buns and fresh hot coffee. Before coming into the room, she sings the St. Lucia song outside the door.

¾ cup milk
⅓ cup plus 2 tablespoons
  sugar
1 teaspoon salt
¼ cup butter
1 teaspoon saffron
2 tablespoons boiling
  water
½ cup warm water

2 packages active dry
  yeast or 2 cakes
  compressed yeast
1 egg, beaten
3 ½ cups sifted flour
  (about)
¼ cup yellow raisins
1 egg white, slightly
  beaten
¼ cup finely chopped
  blanched almonds

Scald milk; stir in ⅓ cup sugar, salt, and butter. Cool to lukewarm. Meanwhile combine saffron and boiling water; let stand. Pour warm water into large mixing bowl. Sprinkle yeast over water; stir until dissolved. Add milk mixture, egg, saffron, and 2 cups of the flour, and beat until smooth. Stir in remaining flour to make soft dough. Turn out on floured surface. Knead with hands until smooth and elastic, about 8 to 10 minutes. Place in greased bowl and turn so that dough will be greased on all sides. Cover and let rise in warm place, free from draft, until doubled in bulk. This takes about 1 hour. Punch down; turn out on floured surface. Cover and let rest 10 minutes.

Set oven at 375° 20 minutes before buns are ready to be baked.

Divide dough into 18 pieces. Roll each piece into a strip of 10 to 12 inches long and cut in half. Coil both ends of each strip into the center of the strip. Place two coiled strips back to back to make one bun. Place on greased baking sheet. Cover and let rise in warm place, free from draft, until doubled in bulk, or about ½ hour. Press a raisin deep into center of each coil. Brush with white of egg. Combine almonds and 2 tablespoons sugar and sprinkle a little on each bun. Bake about 20 minutes.

Finnish May Day Crullers

Tippaleivät

ABOUT 20 CRULLERS

May Day, the First of May, is the Finnish national holiday. Everybody who has ever graduated from high school or college dons his white student cap and gives himself over to frolicking.

The national drink for this day is *sima* (see page 243), and with it are served the following crisp and delicious crullers.

3 eggs
5 tablespoons granulated
  sugar
1 ¾ cups sifted flour

1 cup heavy cream
Fat or oil for
  deep-frying
Confectioners' sugar

Beat eggs with granulated sugar until thick. Alternately stir in flour and heavy cream. Beat until smooth. Heat fat or oil for deep-frying to 380°. Spoon batter into pastry tube. Squeeze batter into fat in a crisscross stream to make a circle the size of a doughnut. Fry on both sides about 2 to 3 minutes or until browned. Drain on paper towels and sprinkle with confectioners' sugar. Serve hot with *sima*.

Swedish Rings

Svensk Punschkakor

½ cup butter or margarine
1 cup sifted flour
2 tablespoons Swedish
  punsch or rum

1 egg, beaten
½ cup finely chopped
  almonds
2 tablespoons sugar

Set oven at 350°.

Cream butter until fluffy. Add flour and Swedish punsch. Mix thoroughly with spoon or with hands. Roll out on waxed paper to strips 4 inches long and ½ inch wide. Shape strips into rings. Brush with egg. Combine almonds and sugar and sprinkle on top of cookies. Bake on buttered and floured cookie sheets for 8 to 10 minutes or until golden.

Rye Rings

Rågkakor

Light and not too sweet, with a hole in the middle.

1 cup butter
½ cup sugar
1 cup sifted rye flour

1 ¼ cups sifted
all-purpose flour

Cream butter and gradually add sugar. Stir in rye flour first; mix thoroughly. Then add all-purpose flour. Chill dough 30 minutes.

Set oven at 350°.

Work with a little of the dough at one time; keep remaining dough in refrigerator until ready to handle. Knead dough slightly and roll out as thin as possible between 2 sheets of waxed paper. Prick surface with fork all over. Cut out rounds with 2- or 3-inch cookie cutter. Cut center from cookies with thimble. Place cookies on buttered and floured cookie sheet, using spatula. Bake about 8 to 10 minutes or until golden. Cool on cookie sheets.

Scandinavian Spritz Cookies or *S* Cookies

A universal Northern European cookie, usually shaped like an *S*.

1 cup butter at room
temperature
⅔ cup sugar
3 egg yolks
1 teaspoon vanilla

2 ½ cups sifted flour
Candied cherries
Vanilla confectioners'
sugar (recipe
below)

Set oven at 375°.

Cream together butter and sugar. Beat in egg yolks, one at

a time. Stir in vanilla. Blend in flour. Force through cookie press or spritz gun into round swirls. Decorate middle with a candied cherry. Or shape into *S*. Bake 7 to 10 minutes or until golden. Sprinkle with vanilla confectioners' sugar.

VANILLA CONFECTIONERS' SUGAR

Combine 2 cups sifted confectioners' sugar and 1 vanilla bean. Place in container with tight lid, and store, covered, for 2 days or longer before using.

Norwegian Pepper Nuts

Peppernøtter

A wonderful old-fashioned recipe from the family of Kaptein Sverre Holck of the Bergen Line, who ran a fine and most abundant table on his ship.

1/3 cup butter
3 1/2 cups confectioners'
* sugar*
4 eggs, beaten
4 to 5 tablespoons
* lemon juice*
1 tablespoon grated
* lemon rind*
1/4 cup chopped candied
* orange peel*
1/2 cup chopped candied
* lemon peel*
1/2 cup chopped candied
* citron*
4 cups sifted flour

1 teaspoon ground
* cinnamon*
1 teaspoon ground
* cloves*
3/4 teaspoon black
* pepper*
1 teaspoon aniseed
1 teaspoon ground
* allspice*
1 tablespoon ground
* cardamom*
1 teaspoon baking soda
1 teaspoon salt
1/2 teaspoon almond
* extract*

Cream butter and gradually add 2½ cups confectioners' sugar. Beat in eggs and blend thoroughly. Stir in 3 tablespoons lemon juice, lemon rind, orange and lemon peels, and citron. Sift flour with remaining ingredients except almond extract. Add to fruit mixture and stir in almond extract. Blend thoroughly. Shape into 1-inch balls and place on greased and floured cookie sheets. Chill overnight.

Set oven at 350°.

Bake pepper nuts about 15 minutes or until browned. While still warm, brush with lemon icing, made by stirring 1 to 2 tablespoons lemon juice into 1 cup sifted confectioners' sugar and stirring to spreading consistency.

NOTE: The pepper nuts should be shaped before chilling or the dough will be too stiff to handle.

Old-Fashioned Scandinavian
Sour Cream Cookies

The recipe can easily be doubled.

½ cup butter
¾ cup sugar
1 egg
2 ¼ cups sifted flour
½ teaspoon baking
 soda
½ teaspoon baking
 powder

½ teaspoon salt
1 teaspoon ground
 cardamom or
 grated nutmeg
½ cup sour cream
Vanilla confectioners'
 sugar (see page 225)

Cream butter and gradually add sugar. Beat in egg. Sift flour with baking soda, baking powder, salt, and cardamom. Stir into butter mixture alternately with sour cream, beginning and ending with flour. Chill overnight or until firm enough to roll.

Set oven at 375°.

Roll dough on floured board to about ¼-inch thickness. Cut with round 3-inch cookie cutter. Bake on ungreased cookie sheets about 12 minutes or until golden brown. Sprinkle with vanilla confectioners' sugar.

Scandinavian Almond Cookies

These very good cookies are a typical example of the rich, buttery cookies beloved by Scandinavians.

1 ¼ cups shelled almonds, blanched or unblanched, according to your taste
1 cup unsalted butter
½ cup sugar

1 teaspoon vanilla or grated rind of 1 large lemon
½ teaspoon salt
2 cups sifted flour
Vanilla confectioners' sugar (see page 225)

Grind almonds fine in nut grinder or electric blender. Cream butter and gradually add sugar. Stir in almonds, vanilla or lemon rind, salt, and flour. Chill for about 2 hours.

Set oven at 350°.

Snip off small pieces of dough and shape into little loaves 1 inch long and ½ inch wide, or into tiny rings, or into crescents. Bake on buttered and floured baking sheets about 15 minutes or until cookies are beginning to be golden. They must not brown. Cool about 3 minutes. Dip in vanilla sugar.

Scandinavian Almond Macaroons

Makroner

½ pound almond paste
(about 1 cup)
(see page 194)
1 cup sifted confectioners'
sugar

½ teaspoon vanilla
½ teaspoon salt
2 to 3 egg whites
Granulated sugar

Set oven at 300°.

Knead almond paste until soft; work in sugar. Add vanilla and salt. Add egg whites, a little at a time, blending well after each addition. Use just enough egg whites to make a soft dough that will hold its shape when dropped from a teaspoon. Line cookie sheets with unglazed brown paper. Drop paste onto sheets by teaspoonfuls, about 2 inches apart. Or force through a cookie press into rounds. Sprinkle with granulated sugar. Bake about 20 minutes. Place macaroons on damp towel to loosen the brown paper, and remove paper. Cool on racks.

Danish Almond Paste Cookies

The colored icing sugar can be bought in any market where sprinkles and other cake decorations are sold.

1 cup butter
¼ pound almond paste
(see page 194)
½ cup superfine sugar

1 egg, beaten
2 cups sifted flour
⅛ teaspoon salt
Colored icing sugar

Set oven at 375°.

Cream butter with almond paste. Beat in sugar gradually; add egg. Stir in flour sifted with salt. Mix thoroughly. Shape through cookie press in the shape of daisies. Fill centers with colored icing sugar. Bake 10 to 15 minutes or until golden.

Swedish Dream Cookies

Drömmar

They are made extra crisp and flaky by the ammonium carbonate used in lieu of baking powder. (See notes on page 175.)

1 cup butter	1 teaspoon pulverized
½ cup sugar	ammonium carbonate
½ teaspoon vanilla	(hartshorn salt)
2 cups sifted flour	½ cup blanched
	almonds

Cream butter and gradually add sugar. Stir in vanilla. Sift flour with ammonium carbonate and add to butter mixture. Blend thoroughly. Chill dough for 1 hour.

Set oven at 350°.

Snip off small pieces of dough and roll into balls the size of a jumbo olive. Place on greased and floured baking sheets. Press down center with finger tip and place one whole almond or half an almond in each center. Bake about 12 to 15 minutes or until golden brown.

Finnish Bread

Finskbrød

Popular throughout Scandinavia, and an excellent, light cookie.

1 cup sifted flour
⅛ teaspoon salt
¼ cup plus 3 tablespoons
* sugar*
½ cup ground
* unblanched almonds*

½ cup butter
1 egg white,
* slightly beaten*
⅓ cup chopped
* almonds*

In mixing bowl combine flour, salt, ¼ cup sugar, and ground almonds. Cut in butter with pastry cutter or two knives. Stir mixture into a soft dough and divide into four parts. Chill 15 minutes. Set oven at 350°. With floured hands roll out the four parts of dough into four ½-inch-wide flat or round strips. The strips must be of even length. On floured surface place strips parallel to each other. With sharp knife and using ruler as a guide, cut through all 4 strips at one time making 1½-inch pieces. Place cookies on buttered and floured cookie sheets. Brush with egg white. Combine chopped almonds and 3 tablespoons sugar and sprinkle over cookies. Bake 10 to 12 minutes or until golden. Cool on cookie sheets and remove carefully.

Swedish Cinnamon Cookies

Kanelkakor

These cookies are not the usual Central European cinnamon stars, which are made with egg white. They are very tender and flavorful cookies.

<table>
<tr><td>⅔ cup butter</td><td>1 ⅓ cups sifted flour</td></tr>
<tr><td>1 cup sugar</td><td>1 teaspoon baking
   powder</td></tr>
<tr><td>1 egg</td><td></td></tr>
<tr><td>1 teaspoon vanilla</td><td>1 teaspoon ground
   cinnamon</td></tr>
</table>

TOPPING

<table>
<tr><td>½ cup walnuts, finely
   chopped</td><td>2 tablespoons ground
   cinnamon
2 tablespoons sugar</td></tr>
</table>

Cream butter and gradually add sugar. Beat in egg and vanilla. Sift flour with baking powder and cinnamon. Add to egg mixture and blend thoroughly. Chill for 30 minutes.

Set oven at 350°.

Combine walnuts, cinnamon, and sugar for topping. Roll chilled dough into balls the size of walnuts. Roll each ball into walnut-cinnamon sugar. Place cookies on greased and floured baking sheets about 3 inches apart. Bake 12 minutes.

All-Scandinavian Honey Cookies

Store for 2 weeks in an airtight container before using—but they will keep for much longer.

1 cup honey
1 cup sugar
2 tablespoons lemon juice
1 tablespoon chopped
candied citron
1 tablespoon chopped
candied lemon peel
1 tablespoon chopped
candied orange peel
2 ⅔ cups blanched
almonds

2 cups sifted flour
¼ teaspoon ground
cinnamon
¼ teaspoon ground
cloves
¼ teaspoon grated
nutmeg
½ teaspoon ground
cardamom

LEMON ICING

About 2 tablespoons
lemon juice

1 cup sifted
confectioners' sugar

Heat honey, but do not boil. Stir in sugar, lemon juice, citron, and lemon and orange peels. Grind 2 cups of the almonds in a nut grinder or an electric blender. Add almonds to fruit mixture. Sift flour with spices. Add to fruits and blend thoroughly. Cover and chill 3 days.

Set oven at 325°.

On floured board, roll out dough very thin. Cut with cookie

cutters into any desired shapes. Bake on greased and floured cookie sheets 8 to 10 minutes. Cool.

Meanwhile, make lemon icing. Stir lemon juice into confectioners' sugar. Beat until of spreading consistency. Spread cookies with icing. Place 1 almond from remaining almonds on each cookie.

Grandmother's Jelly Cookies

Mormor's Syltkakor

A traditional Swedish Christmas cookie, consisting of a large cookie topped with a smaller one.

½ cup butter, at room
    temperature
⅓ cup plus 2 tablespoons
    sugar
1 egg, separated
1 ¼ cups sifted flour

¼ teaspoon salt
2 tablespoons finely
    chopped blanched
    almonds
Currant jelly

Set oven at 375°.

Cream butter and gradually add ⅓ cup sugar. Beat in egg yolk, flour, and salt. Blend thoroughly. On floured surface roll out dough to about ¼-inch thickness. (The dough must be thin.) Divide dough in half. Cut one portion of the dough with 2⅓-inch round cookie cutter. Cut the other portion of the dough with a round or scalloped 2-inch cookie cutter. Remove center of 2-inch cookies with a thimble. Beat egg white slightly. Combine almonds and 2 tablespoons sugar. Brush each 2-inch cookie (those with the hole) with egg white and sprinkle with almond-sugar mixture. Place on buttered and floured cookie sheets almond side up. Bake all cookies about 6 to 8 minutes. Do not let brown. Cool cookies on racks. Place about ½ teaspoon currant jelly on bigger cookie and top with smaller cookie, almond side up. The jelly should appear in the hole in the center of the top cookie.

Lacy Swedish Almond Wafers

Mandelflarn

These are usually served with a custard or with a molded dessert.

¾ cup unblanched
   almonds, finely ground
½ cup unsalted butter, at
   room temperature
½ cup sugar

1 tablespoon flour
⅛ teaspoon salt
2 tablespoons heavy
   cream

Set oven at 350°.

Combine all ingredients in small heavy saucepan. Heat until butter melts, stirring constantly. Drop by teaspoonfuls on buttered and floured cookie sheet, about 4 inches apart. Don't bake more than 6 cookies at one time. Bake about 7 minutes or until edges are browning but center is still bubbly. Cool 1 minute. Loosen each cookie with a sharp knife and wrap immediately around the handle of a wooden spoon. Cool on racks joint side down. These cookies are very fragile and must be handled carefully.

NOTE: If cookies are too crisp to remove from cookie sheet, return to oven for a few seconds. These cookies can also be kept flat and sandwiched with any favorite filling.

Norwegian Berliner Kranser

Scandinavians decorate their cookies with sparkling pearl sugar. The nearest approach to pearl sugar in America is crushed sugar cubes. They will sparkle in a way not even approximated by ordinary sugar. To crush sugar cubes, place them in a paper bag and hit them with a hammer. This way, the sugar won't fly all over the kitchen.

1 hard-cooked egg yolk
1 raw egg yolk
½ cup confectioners' sugar
½ teaspoon vanilla
1 ¾ cups sifted flour

½ cup butter, at room temperature
1 egg white, slightly beaten
Sparkling sugar

Combine hard-cooked and raw egg yolks and blend to a smooth paste; beat in sugar and vanilla. Work in flour and cut in butter. Mix thoroughly; this is best done by hand. Chill 4 hours.

Set oven at 350°.

Snip off small pieces of dough and roll between hands into strips, about 7 inches long and ½ inch thick. If dough sticks, flour hands. Shape strips into rings, looping ends, and let ends overlap a little. Brush with egg white and sprinkle with sugar. Bake about 8 to 10 minutes. These cookies must not brown.

Swedish Almond Rusks

Mandelskorpar

A pleasant plain cookie.

⅓ cup butter
¾ cup sugar
2 eggs
½ teaspoon vanilla
½ teaspoon almond
extract

⅔ cup blanched
almonds, coarsely
chopped
1 ¾ cups sifted flour
1 ½ teaspoons baking
powder

Set oven at 375°.

Cream butter and sugar until light. Beat in eggs, one at a time; then add vanilla and almond extracts and almonds. Blend until smooth. Sift together flour and baking powder and stir gradually into batter. Butter and flour cookie sheets. Spread batter in 1½-inch-wide strips. Bake 8 to 10 minutes or until golden. Remove from oven and cut immediately into ½-inch slices. Turn off oven and return cookies to dry out for about 15 minutes.

BREADS

Swedish Shrove Tuesday Buns

Semlor

10 TO 12 BUNS

Traditionally served on Shrove Tuesday and throughout Lent.
These large light buns are good with coffee, though in Sweden
they are often accompanied by hot milk with cinnamon.

1 package dry yeast
¼ cup lukewarm water
1 egg, slightly beaten
⅔ cup light cream,
  lukewarm
¼ cup granulated sugar
¼ teaspoon salt
½ teaspoon ground
  cinnamon

½ cup butter, at room
  temperature
3 to 3 ¼ cups sifted
  flour
Almond paste (see
  note)
Whipped cream
Confectioners' sugar

Sprinkle yeast on warm water and stir until dissolved. Stir in
half of the beaten egg (reserve other half), lukewarm cream,
granulated sugar, salt, cinnamon, and butter. Mix thoroughly.
Add flour, a little at a time, and beat to make a soft dough. Turn
out dough on floured surface and knead about 10 minutes, or

238 / CLASSIC SCANDINAVIAN COOKING

until dough is smooth and elastic. Place dough in greased bowl and turn to grease on all sides. Cover and let rise until double in bulk, or about 1 to 1½ hours. Punch down risen dough and knead on floured board until smooth. Shape dough into 10 or 12 round buns. Place buns on greased cookie sheet. Let rise until almost double in size. Set oven at 400° 20 minutes before buns are ready to be baked. Brush with reserved egg. Bake 10 to 12 minutes or until golden brown. Cool on racks. Cut off tops of buns with a sharp knife. Insert a wafer-thin piece of almond paste into each bun. Top with whipped cream. Replace top of bun and sprinkle with confectioners' sugar.

NOTE: Almond paste is available in gourmet stores, or see recipe page 194.

Swedish Rye Bread

A very good, easy bread.

1 cup milk	1 teaspoon fennel seed
1 package dry yeast or	1 teaspoon aniseed
1 cake compressed	⅓ cup butter or
yeast	margarine
2 tablespoons sugar	Grated rind of 1 orange
Lukewarm water	1 ½ teaspoons salt
4 ½ cups all-purpose flour	3 cups medium rye
¾ cup dark corn syrup	flour

Scald milk and cool to lukewarm. Dissolve yeast and sugar in 1 cup lukewarm water and stir in milk. Beat in 3 cups flour. Cover and let rise until double in bulk, or about 1 to 1½ hours.

Combine syrup, fennel, and anise in saucepan and bring to boiling point. Cool to lukewarm. Beat syrup, butter, orange rind, and salt into risen batter. Stir in rye flour and 1 cup of the remaining flour. Use remaining ¼ cup flour for kneading. Sprinkle some of ¼ cup flour on bread board and turn dough on it. Knead with floured hands until smooth and elastic. Place in greased bowl, turn to grease on all sides, and let rise until double in bulk, from ½ to 2 hours.

Shape dough into 2 loaves. Grease two 9- × 5-inch bread loaf pans, and place loaves in pans. Cover and let rise until double in bulk, or about 50 minutes.

Set oven at 375°.

Bake loaves about 45 minutes. Brush with lukewarm water and bake 5 minutes longer.

Finnish Brown Bread

Hiivaleipä

The Finnish country people are great bakers. The old-time ovens used to be built into the wall behind the stove like a tunnel, about a yard wide and sometimes as deep as six feet. At baking time, a wood fire was lit in the oven, and when it had burned down to red and glowing embers, these were raked forward into the stove with a long pole that ended in a kind of iron shovel. The oven was then cleaned with a broom dipped in water. A ventilator at the back of the stove drew off the smoke, and was closed as the fire was raked out. A damper regulated the heat.

Since heating an oven was a time-consuming business, the Finnish farm wives baked in large quantities. The following bread has a textured grain and a light brown color. The shape is round, and it is eaten cut in wedges, which are split and buttered. The bread also toasts extremely well.

1 ½ cups hot water
2 tablespoons butter, at
  room temperature
1 tablespoon sugar
2 teaspoons salt
1 package dry yeast
½ cup lukewarm
  water

3 cups whole-wheat
  or rye flour
2 ½ cups unsifted
  all-purpose flour
  (about)
Melted butter

Pour hot water into a large mixing bowl. Stir in butter, sugar, and salt. Cool to lukewarm. Stir yeast into lukewarm water and dissolve completely. Add to first mixture and blend well. Beat in whole-wheat or rye flour. Add 2 cups all-purpose flour. Use remaining ½ cup to flour pastry board. Turn dough onto floured pastry board and knead 10 minutes. Add more flour to board if dough sticks, but only a little at a time. Knead until dough is smooth and satiny. Grease a large bowl and place dough in it. Brush top with melted butter. Cover with a lightly dampened kitchen towel. Allow to rise in a warm place (85°) about 45 minutes to 1 hour or until almost doubled in bulk. Twenty minutes before time is up set oven at 400°. Punch down dough and divide into 2 halves. Grease a baking sheet. Form each half of dough into a round loaf. Place on baking sheet; press down with hands until the loaf is about 1 inch thick. Bake about 30 minutes or until the crust of the bread is light brown. Remove from baking sheet and cool on racks.

Finnish Viipuri Twist

1 VERY LARGE TWIST

A Finnish coffee bread baked in the shape of an enormous pretzel. It is said that the first Viipuri twist was baked for Christmas in a Finnish monastery in 1433. The twist, which is as large as a cookie sheet, is not only outstandingly decorative and most unusual, but also delightful to eat. At Christmas time it is served filled with gingerbread men and other cookies.

1 package dry yeast
¼ cup lukewarm water
¼ teaspoon salt
1 egg, well beaten
7 tablespoons sugar
¾ cup lukewarm milk
2 tablespoons butter,
  at room temperature

¼ teaspoon grated
  nutmeg
½ teaspoon ground
  cardamom
4 cups sifted flour
Boiling water

Sprinkle yeast on lukewarm water and stir until dissolved. Add salt, beaten egg, sugar, lukewarm milk, and butter. Beat in nutmeg and cardamom. Beat in flour gradually to make stiff dough. Knead dough until smooth and elastic. Place dough in a greased bowl. Cover and let rise in warm place until doubled in bulk. Punch down and knead well. Shape dough into a 36-inch-long roll. The middle of the roll should be ½ inch thicker than the ends. Place roll of dough on a greased and floured cookie sheet. Shape dough into twist on the cookie sheet. Keeping the shape of a pretzel in mind, twist both ends of the roll around each other and turn inwards to form the middle of the twist. Separate the ends again and join each on either side of the thick part of the roll, to form a triangular opening in the middle of the twist. Brush with boiling water. Let rise 1 hour.

Just 20 minutes before the hour is up, set oven at 350°.

Brush twist with boiling water again and place in oven. Bake 40 to 50 minutes or until twist is deep brown. Remove from oven and brush again with boiling water.

DRINKS

Finnish Sima, the May Day Drink

ABOUT 1 GALLON

May Day, the First of May, is a great Finnish holiday with general rejoicing throughout the country. The students put on their traditional white caps, badge of their academic status, and dance, sing, and drink *sima* with their May Day crullers.

Sima is a pleasant, slightly acidic, and refreshing drink. This recipe can be doubled or tripled.

1 lemon	One 12-ounce can beer
4 quarts water	or 2 tablespoons
2 cups plus 2 teaspoons	hops
sugar	¼ teaspoon dry yeast
2 cups light brown	Raisins
sugar	

With a sharp knife pare off the yellow part of the lemon rind and reserve. Peel off the white part and throw away. Slice the lemon and remove seeds. In a large kettle or enameled bucket combine water, 2 cups each of the sugars, lemon slices, and lemon peel. Bring mixture to a boil. Remove from heat and add beer or hops. When mixture has cooled to lukewarm, dissolve yeast in ½ cup of mixture and stir into brew. Cover tightly and let stand overnight at room temperature. Strain *sima*. Prepare 4 quart bottles by rinsing them with boiling water. Place ½ teaspoon sugar and 3 to 4 raisins in each bottle. Fill bottle with *sima* and cap. Store in a cool place. The *sima* is ready when the raisins have risen to the surface. Serve chilled.

Swedish Punsch

Svensk Punsch

ABOUT 1 ¾ GALLONS

An old-fashioned drink, with a sweet, innocent taste that lures the unwary to underestimate its potency. There are many recipes for it, though nowadays it is usually bought ready bottled. Whatever the recipe, Swedish punsch must contain arrack. The following recipe, from Inga Norberg's *Good Food from Sweden*, is a good one.

4 ½ quarts water	1 bottle 100 proof
5 ½ pounds sugar	vodka
2 bottles arrack	2 teaspoons glycerine
1 bottle Cognac	

In large heavy kettle boil together water and sugar to make 4½ quarts syrup. Cool. Stir in all other ingredients. Continue stirring punch for ¾ to 1 hour. Bottle in 7 quart bottles; cork and seal bottles. Store bottles lying on their sides. The punch improves with time, but it can be served after 5 days. Serve ice cold.

Swedish Glögg

ABOUT 2 QUARTS

No Swedish Christmas is complete without plenty of *glögg*. It certainly is a heart-and-body warming drink.

3 whole cardamom pods
8 whole cloves
1 cinnamon stick
One 4-inch strip of orange
   rind (yellow part only)
1 ⅓ cups water

¼ cup blanched
   almonds
½ cup golden raisins
1 bottle Bordeaux wine
1 bottle port wine
½ bottle Cognac
Sugar to taste

Tie cardamom pods, cloves, cinnamon, and orange rind in a cheesecloth bag. Place in the water and bring to a boil. Simmer, covered, 10 minutes. Add almonds and raisins and simmer 10 minutes longer. Add Bordeaux wine, port wine, and Cognac and bring to a quick boil. Remove from heat immediately. Cool and store, covered, overnight. At serving time, remove spice bag. Heat *glögg* but do not boil. Add sugar to taste. Serve in heated mugs or glasses, with a few almonds and raisins in each glass.

INDEX